STRATEGIC CC
AT WORK

Strategic Communication at Work provides the reader with a practical approach to engaging in all types of communication—one-on-one, small group, and large group—to achieve intended results. The framework presented enables readers to make informed decisions that increase the effectiveness of their communication and enhance their credibility.

Lennard presents the IMPACT Paradigm—Intending, Messaging, Presence, Attending, Connecting, and Together—in the first part of the book, explaining the benefits of using a single framework for all strategic communication. The second part illustrates how to apply these principles and approach interactions with a purposeful mindset, express ideas congruently, and connect with others. The third part offers curated exercises for practicing communication skills, along with specific ways to integrate the paradigm into everyday communication interactions.

The text's clear and practical approach will appeal to graduate students of business communication, as well as instructors and professionals interested in improving their communication skills.

Diane Lennard, PhD, is a Professor of Management Communication at Stern School of Business, New York University, USA. She is also the founder of Lennard & Company, an international coaching and consulting firm specializing in experiential learning programs for business executives, educators, consultants, and other professionals.

STRATEGIC COMMUNICATION AT WORK

The IMPACT Paradigm

Diane Lennard

Routledge
Taylor & Francis Group

NEW YORK AND LONDON

First published 2018
by Routledge
711 Third Avenue, New York, NY 10017

and by Routledge
2 Park Square, Milton Park, Abingdon, Oxon, OX14 4RN

Routledge is an imprint of the Taylor & Francis Group, an informa business

Library of Congress Cataloging-in-Publication Data
A catalog record for this book has been requested

ISBN: 978-1-138-71459-5 (hbk)
ISBN: 978-1-138-71462-5 (pbk)
ISBN: 978-1-315-23078-8 (ebk)

Typeset in Bembo and Stone Sans
by Florence Production Ltd, Stoodleigh, Devon, UK

CONTENTS

PREFACE

This book is about how we communicate to achieve intended results. It is based on the idea that we can apply the same basic communication principles to one-on-one, small group, and large group situations at work. Based on my experience as a performer, communication coach, and management communication professor, I have distilled a set of interconnected principles that enable people to engage in interactions that achieve their goals. In this book, I organize these basic strategic communication principles into one cohesive framework—the IMPACT Paradigm.

The use of one framework for thinking about all strategic communication benefits students who would like to refine their communication skills and gain a competitive advantage in the workplace, and professionals who interact daily with others and want to achieve better results. The IMPACT Paradigm offers a practical approach to communicating effectively with individuals and groups at work.

Students and professionals who want to become more effective strategic communicators can apply the paradigm principles to any interaction. They can use the IMPACT Paradigm to express their ideas more succinctly, persuade others more successfully, engage their audiences with more confidence, and communicate more effectively to achieve their goals working with, and through, other people.

In *Strategic Communication at Work: The IMPACT Paradigm*, I explain why establishing mutual engagement, expressing authentic messages, and focusing on intended outcomes are necessary for having the impact we want on individuals and groups. While writing this book, I make every effort to stay focused on my intended outcome—what specifically I want as a result of this written communication. I want readers to understand the basic principles of the paradigm, apply the principles to their unique communication challenges at work, and know how to practice so they can continually improve their communication effectiveness. To this end, I divide the book into three parts.

Part One provides an overview of the IMPACT Paradigm. Chapter 1 introduces each of the six interrelated principles of the paradigm: **I**ntending, **M**essaging, **P**resence, **A**ttending, **C**onnecting, **T**ogether. Chapter 2 explores the paradigm more deeply, with particular attention paid to the benefits of using one framework for all strategic communication.

Part Two illustrates how strategic communicators can apply the principles and approach interactions with an impact mindset. Chapter 3 describes nine examples of work situations, demonstrating how the paradigm principles have been put into action. Chapter 4 considers how communicators can reframe common concerns and limiting beliefs by adopting an impact mindset.

Part Three focuses on practice. I offer curated exercises for practicing communication skills, using the IMPACT Paradigm, and facilitating continual improvement in communication effectiveness. Chapter 5 gives detailed instructions for IMPACT Exercises that help people prepare for interactions, polish and refine skills, and communicate with impact. Chapter 6 suggests a variety of ways to approach practice and integrate the paradigm into everyday communication interactions.

ACKNOWLEDGMENTS

I'd like to thank all of the people who made this book possible. Special thanks to:

- Jessy Hsieh, who formalized this framework with me, read and responded thoughtfully to every chapter, asked insightful questions and listened carefully during invigorating review sessions, contributed in countless ways to my thinking process, and added an indispensable perspective, all while teaching and writing her PhD dissertation.

- Tita Beal and Shana Carroll, who read drafts, provided feedback, and offered vital support along the way.

- Jenn Wynn, Lindsey Dietschi, Charlie Murphy, Bryan Coughlin, Ellen Mednick, Dan Ebersole, Jim Romanelli, Anne Gregory, Beth Briggs, Jenny Hershey, Maria Arnone, and Dianne McGuire, who provided valuable input.

- Davina Lennard Alladice, who designed the graphics and inspires me every day.

- The clients of Lennard & Company, who contributed to the development of many of the ideas in this book.

- The students, faculty, and administrators at NYU Stern, NYU Langone Medical School, Yale Law School, and Yale Institute for Social and Policy Studies, with whom I've had the privilege of working with and learning from during coaching sessions, workshops, and classes.

PART ONE

Strategic Communication

1

THE IMPACT PARADIGM—
WHAT IT IS

We all communicate. At work, we engage in purposeful, goal-directed communication. Strategic communication, the purposeful use of communication interactions to achieve intended goals and outcomes, is for everyone.

All of us set out to communicate in ways that are relevant to the goals we want to achieve, but sometimes we face challenges along the way.

Ever been in any of these communication situations?

- Proposing a new plan—How can I gain agreement?

- Speaking in a meeting—How can I express my thoughts clearly and succinctly?

- Presenting to a new group of people—How can I get, and hold, the group's attention?

- Updating clients—How can I convey confidence and conviction in my ideas?

- Negotiating a contract—How can I create a trusting relationship and achieve a great result?

- Interviewing for a job—How can I connect with the interviewer and have a genuine conversation?

- Networking—How can I come across as competent and valuable?

- Delivering a keynote speech—How can I engage the entire audience?

Our success in these interactions depends on our ability to communicate effectively to achieve results. We all know things can go awry—getting nervous, becoming distracted, feeling unprepared, losing confidence, failing to engage others. Based on many years of experience as a communication coach and professor of graduate-level communication courses, I also know we can overcome the obstacles that get in our way.

By applying certain basic principles, we can make informed decisions that will enhance the effectiveness and success of our strategic communication. We can be purposeful throughout an interaction, express our ideas congruently, and enhance our credibility. We can align what we think, say, and do. We can connect with others and engage in dynamic interactions. All of us can communicate with impact and get the results we want.

In this first chapter, we will examine six communication principles that are connected to each other in an integrated way. Together, they form a framework for thinking about strategic communication. This framework is called "The IMPACT Paradigm" because it provides us with a practical approach to communication that has the impact on listeners that we want.

The basic principles of the IMPACT Paradigm are being applied in businesses, legal and medical practices, and academic settings. These concepts serve as the foundation for strategic communication. As we will see in the examples and exercises throughout this book, the paradigm can work across professional contexts and address common communication concerns.

A systems thinking approach informs this paradigm. Strategic communication is a dynamic and complex process of highly integrated components that interact to achieve a desired goal, outcome, or result. To streamline this complexity, we focus on how adjustments made to any one of these interacting components affect both the process of communication and its outcomes. In this approach, we look at how the six principles of the IMPACT Paradigm work together to clarify, guide, and facilitate our communication:

- **Intending:** Identify desired outcomes
- **Messaging:** Convey thoughts and feelings congruently
- **Presence:** Use fullest expression
- **Attending:** Focus out
- **Connecting:** Establish and maintain mutual engagement
- **Together:** Co-create a conversational interaction

Each principle relates to the others and applying them together is essential for making purposeful communication effective.

APPLYING THE IMPACT PARADIGM

The IMPACT Paradigm is a communication framework consisting of six key principles. Applying these paradigm principles will enhance your ability to communicate with impact and get the results you want.

1. **I**ntending:
   Identify what you want to bring about as a result of your communication and then direct your actions toward attaining that desired outcome. Every time you communicate, determine the specific response you want to cause related to what listeners know, how they feel, or ways they act.

2. **M**essaging:
   Convey your thoughts and feelings using three modes of expression—body, voice, and words. A small deliberate change to one aspect of messaging positively affects all the others and can significantly improve your communication. To make an impact, you need to make sure your visual, vocal, and verbal communication all support each other.

3. **P**resence:
   Consider how you show up, including how you hold physical space and how you hold attention with

your voice. You can increase your presence.
This involves taking actions that move you toward
the goal of developing your fullest expression
of self.

4. **A**ttending:
   Focus out, attentively watch, and actively listen to the
   people with whom you are communicating. With
   individuals and groups, the action is the same: get
   each thought out of your head and direct your full
   attention to the person receiving your message;
   complete a thought with that person before moving
   on to speak to another person.

5. **C**onnecting:
   Apply two principles together, attending and
   connecting, to establish and maintain mutual
   engagement. Connecting extends the relationship
   that attending has accomplished and activates a
   shared focus. Speaker and listener engage as
   co-participants in the communication.

6. **T**ogether
   Create shared meaning, reach outcomes, and
   take informed action with others through
   conversational interactions. These dynamic and
   collaborative interactions involve speaking and listening,
   paying attention to verbal and non-verbal
   communication, understanding and engaging—
   together.

Principle 1: Intending

When we identify what we want to bring about as a result of our communication and then direct our actions toward attaining that desired outcome, we are applying the principle of intending. Every time we communicate we affect the people with whom we are communicating; and therefore, it is critically important to determine what response we specifically want to cause in them. That response can relate to what they know, how they feel, or ways they act.

An intention is defined in the *American Heritage Dictionary* as "an aim that guides action." At work, we need to know what we want to accomplish when we deliver our messages. Goal achievement becomes a hit-or-miss activity when we talk without having a focus on, or strong commitment to, attaining a desired outcome. We may achieve our outcome but we also may not. For this reason, it is crucial that we begin the process of communication with intending—knowing the effect we want to cause in others and setting that as a goal for each interaction. In other words, I recommend beginning with the end in mind.

Not only must we determine our desired outcome, we must also convey that outcome to those with whom we are communicating. According to research in the field of neuroscience, mirror neurons, "collections of special cells in the brain [that] bind us with each other, mentally and emotionally" (Iacoboni 2008, 4), provide one explanation for how others understand the meaning of our intentions. Daniel Goleman, author of *Emotional Intelligence* (1997) and *Social Intelligence* (2006), believes that social skill (the ability to recognize, manage, and influence the feelings of others) depends on multiple mirror neuron systems in the brain that mimic actions, read emotions, and read intentions. These special cells create a shared sensibility by mimicking what another person does or feels: "This triggering of parallel circuitry in two brains lets us instantly achieve a shared sense of what counts in a given moment" (Goleman 2006, 43).

This research shows that having a clear intention is crucial because that intention will be perceived by others. We convey our intention through physical and vocal communication behaviors, known as intention cues. People read and respond to these intention cues. It is imperative that the cues we send with our facial expressions, voice, and body language align with our words so our intention can be understood. When mixed signals are sent, people can become confused. For example, people who smile while speaking about serious issues most likely give cues that are picked up incorrectly by others and undermine their intent.

"With the attention to intention we develop an integrated state of coherence" (Siegel 2007, 206). This is a key concept: focusing on a clear intention naturally results in bringing our physical, vocal, and verbal communication in sync and in support of our identified intention.

By firmly focusing on and congruently expressing a clear intention throughout a communication, listeners can understand the purpose of the message and respond to it. There is no guarantee that we'll always get our intended outcome. However, by maintaining a strong intention, our listeners will know what we want from them, and the likelihood we will get that response significantly increases.

Intending and congruent message delivery go hand in hand.

Principle 2: Messaging

When we apply the principle of messaging, we convey our thoughts and feelings using three modes of expression—body, voice, and words. Speaking is a physical act, as well as a vocal and verbal one. To make an impact, we need to make sure that our visual, vocal, and verbal communication all support each other. What does this mean?

First, consider how we express ourselves using visual communication—what others see. Our messages are conveyed through body language, including head movements, facial expressions, hand gestures, physical posture, eye contact, muscle tensions and breathing patterns. The position of our bodies in physical space and our movements send non-verbal signals to the people with whom we are communicating. Two dimensions of non-verbal communication are particularly relevant to communication interactions at work: kinesics (behavior related to movement of the hand, arm, face, or the body as a whole) and proxemics (how use of space and distance influence communication).

Second, consider our vocal communication—how we sound to others. This is called paralanguage, and refers to the elements of speech aside from the words themselves that we use to convey shades of meaning. These include speaking pace, pitch, volume, intonation, tone, pronunciation, pauses, and articulation. All of these paralinguistic cues express our attitude, emotion, and meaning to listeners.

Third, there is our verbal communication—what words we choose to say. Storytelling, for example, can be an engaging, effective way to convey memorable verbal messages. Stories are often relatable and emotional. When stories are structured with a clear beginning, middle, and end, they are logically and psychologically satisfying for listeners. Short sentences with precise words, especially when each sentence is followed by a pause, give people time to process what was just said. Using concrete, visually dynamic words and phrases enriches our verbal communication. "Words and imagery provide clues to the meanings and the important values, assumptions, and experiences that lie behind a person's choice of words" (McCaskey 1979, 137). Every individual word we choose to use matters because it is a verbal symbol that communicates meaning to listeners.

We create, exchange, and share meaning with others through sending and receiving verbal and non-verbal messages. Our non-verbal cues can reinforce, contradict, or modify the words we use. For example, a person can use words to express excitement about an idea and contradict that message by looking and sounding bored, or can reinforce that message with facial expression and tone of voice.

Communication researcher Albert Mehrabian emphasized the importance of non-verbal elements of personal communication, particularly as they relate to sending and receiving feelings or forming attitudes of liking or disliking another person. "Generalizing, we can say that a person's nonverbal behavior has more bearing than his words on communicating feelings or attitudes to others" (Mehrabian 1971, 44). He offered an equation for how we communicate our feelings: 7% words + 38% vocal expressions + 55% facial expressions.

Many communication researchers have confirmed that listeners are much more likely to trust the non-verbal messages over the actual meaning of the speaker's words when there is ambiguity or an obvious mismatch among these elements of communication.

Kinesics, founded by anthropologist Ray Birdwhistell, is the study of body movements, posture, and gestures (Birdwhistell 1970). It looks at how we communicate messages to others by the ways we stand, sit, walk, and move our head, arms, hands, legs, and feet. Kinesic communication, the technical term for body language, also includes eye contact and facial expressions. Consider how much meaning is interpreted from our facial expressions alone. As stated by facial expressions expert Paul Ekman in *Become Versed in Reading Faces*: "In business and in life, it doesn't matter what language you speak, where you live, what you do for a living—the facial expressions you show for anger, fear, sadness, disgust, surprise, contempt and happiness will be the same" (2009, 1). Ekman's studies suggest that the facial expressions of some emotions are universal, shared with all human beings.

Proxemics, how distance and space influence communication and behavior, is another aspect of non-verbal communication. Edward T. Hall, the renowned cultural anthropologist who explored proxemics, wrote in *The Silent Language*: "Spatial changes give a tone to a communication, accent it, and at times, even override the spoken word. The flow and shift of distance between people as they interact with each other is part and parcel of the communication process" (1973, 175). In *The Hidden Dimension*, Hall identified four distance zones used in communication interactions—intimate, personal, social, and public—that vary depending on the proxemic patterns of people in different cultures, personality and environmental factors (1966, 116).

Hall investigated differences in communication styles across cultures and developed the concept of high-context and low-context communication. In *Beyond Culture*, he wrote:

> A high-context (HC) communication or message is one in which most of the information is either in the physical context or internalized in the person, while very little is in the coded, explicit, transmitted part of the message. A low-context (LC) communication is just the opposite; i.e., the mass of the information is vested in the explicit code.
>
> (1976, 91)

According to Hall, meaning in high-context communication is mostly embedded in the context, which includes facial expression, gesture, and tone of voice; whereas meaning in low-context communication is conveyed through the words that are being used. Hall's work suggests that non-verbal signals are especially significant in some intercultural situations, particularly those with people accustomed to high-context communication.

Paralanguage includes all the vocal qualities that accompany speech and contribute to our communication. It refers to how we say things, not what we say. Our vocal qualifiers, often referred to as tone of voice in non-technical terms, are an integral part of every spoken word. We can increase or decrease volume and rate of speech, shorten or elongate individual syllables, raise or lower pitch. All of these non-verbal cues of the voice can modify the meaning of our words.

"We speak with our vocal organs, but we converse with our entire bodies . . ." (Abercrombie 1968, 55). Our verbal messages interact with our non-verbal messages in multiple ways. For example, gestures can emphasize or illustrate a verbal message; tone can influence the meaning of a verbal message; pitch can increase or lessen the intensity of the verbal message.

Sometimes, our verbal and non-verbal cues within the same communication interaction send conflicting messages. When our visual, vocal, and verbal cues do not agree, the result is an unclear message that lacks credibility. For example, an incongruous communication can be caused by a vocal quality or a physical posture that is not in sync with the words spoken, or a mismatch between the facial expressions and the verbal message sent. It also can happen when the speaker's feelings of uncertainty, ambivalence, or even disinterest in conveying a message are expressed through a variety of non-verbal cues.

When our messaging is congruent, it gives the impression that we are confident and have deep conviction in what we are saying. We are perceived as individuals who are sincere, trustworthy, and committed to our intent.

A small deliberate change to one aspect of messaging can positively affect all the others. I recognize in my work with professionals how only a small adjustment to visual, vocal, or verbal expression significantly improves their communication.

Just as messaging requires having all modes of expression in sync, presence involves aligning what we think, say, and do. Messaging and presence are intrinsically related to one another.

Principle 3: Presence

Presence, as it used here, is not the same as charisma—"a divinely conferred power or talent," a magical quality or charm that you either have or do not have, were either gifted with at birth, or not. Instead, I think of presence as how we show up, including how we hold physical space and how we hold attention with our voice. In the IMPACT Paradigm, presence means using our body, voice, and words to fully express our ideas. "When you are not present, people can tell. When you are, people respond" (Cuddy 2015, 21).

Amy Cuddy, social psychologist and professor at Harvard Business School, is well-known for her TED Talk about power poses, "Your body language may shape who you are" (2012). She discussed her research finding that people who adopt certain power positions can change their body chemistry and increase their feelings of power. Cuddy emphasized the mind–body connection: "So it seems that our nonverbals do govern how we think and feel about ourselves, so it's not just others, it's also ourselves. Our bodies change our minds." After receiving tens of millions of personal stories from her TED Talk viewers, she wrote a New York Times bestseller about feeling powerful and becoming more present, *Presence: Bringing Your Boldest Self to Your Biggest Challenges*: "Our search for presence isn't about finding charisma or extraversion or carefully managing the impression we're making on other people. It's about the honest, powerful connection that we create internally with ourselves" (2015, 25). Cuddy believes we can bring on a sense of presence when it escapes us by making small physiological adjustments. She advocates using our body to lead our mind.

Our thoughts and actions are closely linked. They affect how we show up, how we express ourselves, and how we are perceived by others.

> Presence requires alignment between your mind, body, and words—to walk the talk, you need a simultaneous focus on all three levers: mental, skill, and physical. Your presence is an interconnected system of your beliefs and assumptions, your communication skills, and your physical energy.
>
> (Su and Wilkins 2013, 9)

William Kahn, psychologist and Professor of Organizational Behavior at Boston University Questrom School of Business, studied how this kind of alignment of mind, body, and words occurs in an organizational role when performing job-related tasks. In his 1992 article entitled *To Be Fully There: Psychological Presence at Work*, he described four dimensions of psychological presence. They include feeling and being attentive, connected, integrated, and focused. According to Kahn, the first aspect of presence is attentiveness, being open to others; the second aspect is connection, feeling joined with others; the third aspect is integration, being grounded and feeling a sense of wholeness in situations physically, intellectually, and emotionally; and the fourth aspect is focus, using physical, intellectual, and emotional facilities to attend to work and connect with others.

"Psychological presence is most clearly manifested by physical presence" (Kahn 1992, 328). To illustrate this, Kahn described a particular project manager who manifests what he views as "the first level or sense of presence: the person is planted, rooted physically in a way that shows that she is there for the interaction" (329). He considers eye contact the second physical indicator and described in his article how this project manager looked directly at the other person to convey being present to and for him: "She held his gaze and in doing so held him" (329). In addition, he views fullness of speech (para-language) and the words that voices speak as indicators of presence. Kahn described how that same project manager's "voice was filled up with and communicated her personal self: tones, vocal inflections, and pitches varied according to her own patterns of speech" (329). He stated that the project manager's verbal behavior indicated presence by "maintaining dialogues that were on rather than off track" (329). From Kahn's perspective, presence is full expression of self, and he believes that people can improve their presence by bringing deeper levels of themselves to their work situations.

The approach to communicating effectively based on the IMPACT Paradigm holds that we can all increase our presence. It takes awareness, physical stamina, and engagement with the paradigm principles. We are all capable of taking actions that move us toward the goal of developing to our fullest expression of self.

The first three principles of the IMPACT Paradigm focus on expressing ourselves and what we want to achieve as a result of our communication: intending (expressing desired outcomes); messaging (expressing thoughts and feelings congruently); and presence (expressing ourselves more fully, showing up).

The last three IMPACT Paradigm principles focus on interacting with others. These are: attending (focusing attention on others); connecting (establishing and maintaining a connection with others); and together (engaging in a conversational interaction with others).

Principle 4: Attending

Attending to the listener is a vital principle of strategic communication. It requires focusing out, attentively watching and actively listening. With an individual, attending during the interchange of ideas and feelings involves getting each thought out of our head and directing our full attention to that person, while staying fully present and observing the person receiving the message. With groups, the action is the same—a communicator attends to one person at a time, completing a thought with that person before moving on to speak to another person. When addressing a very large group, the speaker attends to a person in a particular area of the room for a complete thought, then moves to another in a different area of the room, and continues this process throughout the communication.

Attendere in Latin literally means "to stretch toward." Definitions of attend from the Oxford Dictionary include: "look after; pay attention to; accompany." When we give all of our physical and cognitive attention to another person, that person will respond in kind and pay attention back. Attending shows that we care about the communication, demonstrated through non-verbal behavior—an involved posture, directly facing the person with whom we are communicating, and direct eye contact. Our focus of attention on the other person signals we are invested in having that person get our message, and, as a consequence, we are involved in a meaningful interaction with that person.

To better understand how attending creates a reciprocal relationship between people, it is useful to examine the meaning of an interactional system from a systems theory perspective on communication. In *Pragmatics of Human Communication*, an interactional system is defined as "two or more communicants in the process of, or at the level of, defining the nature of their relationship" (Watzlawick, Bavelas and Jackson 1967, 121). This places special emphasis on the relationship aspect of communication. Attending to other people facilitates the creation of an interactional system. By focusing attention out on others, they understand our role as communicator and their own as recipient of the communication.

Applying the principle of attending requires shifting from an internal focus to an external focus. Making this shift can sometimes take a concerted effort and at other times can occur by simply remembering to focus out. The great benefit of attending is that it naturally engages others as participants in the communication. It establishes the communication as an interactive process. The speaker and listeners become co-participants. It is the external focus on others that enables us to establish the relational aspect that is needed for communication that works well.

Generally speaking, we understand the importance of attending to the people with whom we are communicating; but all too often we neglect to do so. Why does this happen? It is easy to get caught up in our own thoughts. For some people, this happens when they concentrate on remembering what they were planning to say or get immersed in following their own stream of consciousness. For others, it happens when they focus primarily on self-judgment. These internalized thoughts, as well as the draw of instant access to information from ever-present handheld devices, make it impossible to give full attention to others when speaking and listening. This hinders the process of engaging in a shared, meaningful interaction.

People listen to us when they feel as if we are paying close attention to them—seeing and hearing them. "Attending is giving your physical attention to another person . . . listening with the whole body" (Bolton 1979, 33). Attending makes people feel that they matter and that we get who they are.

It conveys that we care about their needs and interests, and we are reaching out to align with them.

In all communication interactions, attending invites and fosters relatedness with others. Applying the principle of attending makes it possible to establish the kind of reciprocal relationship that is needed for our messages to be received and intended outcomes to be achieved.

Principle 5: Connecting

When we connect with others, the relationship our attending has accomplished is extended and activates a shared focus. It enables the speaker and listener to engage as co-participants in the communication interaction. Once the reciprocal relationship has been established, it is crucial to maintain it. By applying the two principles together, attending and connecting, we establish and maintain connection. We experience how deeply inter-twined these two principles are.

For strategic communication to be successful, it is vitally important to get others to pay attention, continue to pay attention, and fully engage with us and our message. We can create a firm connection with others, what I refer to as a non-negotiable connection, by applying the IMPACT Paradigm principles. Establishing and maintaining a non-negotiable connection secures involvement in the communication interaction and promotes the creation of shared meaning.

Throughout this book, I refer to communication inter-actions. All interactions require two or more people who are connecting with and responding to one another. Attending and connecting are the building blocks of the interactional system in which intending and messaging are expressed. Using the IMPACT Paradigm principles of attending and connecting enables people to share in meaningful communication interactions.

Sherry Turkle, founder and director of the MIT Initiative on Technology, advocated in *Reclaiming Conversation* for making meaning together through in-person conversations: "In conversation, people build trust, get information, and build the connections that help them get their work done" (2015, 284).

Turkle made a compelling case for conversation in a range of different situations. She discussed how some business employers are screening job applicants for their ability to hold a conversation. A vice president at a pharmaceutical company described her hiring strategy:

> Most applicants are prepped for one conversation. And then at the end, I tell the potential recruits that their homework is to organize what we've discussed and from that make an agenda of interesting themes for our next conversation . . . hopefully tomorrow or the day following.
>
> (2015, 46)

Turkle also discussed how the success of professionals in service industries, such as lawyers, accountants, consultants, and bankers, can depend on differentiating themselves from other practitioners in their field: "The best way to avoid being seen as a commodity is to offer a relationship. And that takes conversation" (2015, 288).

It is important to note here that while the IMPACT Paradigm focuses on the connections we make during in-person communication interactions, the principles also apply to a variety of situations online or on the phone. In the digital age that we live in, there are many ways for people to establish and maintain a communication connection. Mutual engagement is essential for all effective strategic communication.

Principle 6: Together

Conversation is derived from Latin words that mean "to move together." By moving together, we build relationships, share information, exchange ideas, and make decisions with others. It is through conversation that we create shared meaning, reach outcomes, and take informed action, together.

In the IMPACT Paradigm, we approach communication as conversational interactions. Let's consider characteristics of effective conversations: familiar, engaging, dynamic, and collaborative.

First, conversations are familiar. We have them all the time. They help us manage the daily flow of giving and receiving information. During a single day at work, we may have planning, reviewing, coaching, managing, evaluating, and decision making conversations with people at many different levels of an organization.

Second, conversations are engaging. They invite mutuality and reciprocity. Conversations often involve a series of exchanges, inquiry, cooperation, and collaboration. Conversations enable us to express existing knowledge and construct new knowledge.

Third, conversations are dynamic. Conversations change as messages are continually added. As conversation participants, we engage in making sense of all the messages that arrive, taking in each one and putting them all together.

Fourth, conversations are a form of collaborative action. We have conversations with others to reach a mutual understanding, called common ground in conversational analysis, and to achieve desired outcomes within a reciprocal relationship.

Grounding is a collaborative process and is essential to ensuring that our messages are appropriately understood. It is a term used in conversational analysis that "refers to the means by which individuals work together to establish mutual beliefs that particular utterances have been understood as intended" (Horton 2012, 384). This perspective sees conversation as a joint activity in which two or more people contribute and acknowledge understanding.

When we communicate with large groups of people, we can create conversational interactions that connect to their concerns and experiences, not just "talk at" them. Even a communication that involves one person speaking to many people can feel as personalized and interactive as a one-on-one conversation. The mutual understanding that occurs during conversational interactions is essential for effective strategic communication.

Our conversational interactions involve speaking and listening, paying attention to verbal and non-verbal communication, understanding and engaging—together.

Conclusion

We can significantly increase the effectiveness of our communication activities at work by combining all six principles of the IMPACT Paradigm. Using the power of three, we can remember the first set of three principles that focuses on our expression (intending, messaging, presence), and the second set of three principles that focuses on our interactions with others (attending, connecting, together).

As we communicate, we can apply these principles to express ourselves, our messages, and our intentions in reciprocal relationships more fully. From a systems perspective, these six principles reinforce one another and form an integrated whole that is greater than the sum of its parts—strategic communication with impact.

Strategic communication requires us to be intentional and responsive. It challenges us to remain goal-directed and to connect with others. It involves our use of communication to inform, influence, and relate. I have stressed that our communication process for building mutual understanding and consensus, and establishing and maintaining mutually beneficial relationships, must be participatory and interactive.

By definition, strategic communication cannot be random. While there are no guarantees that our communication activities will be successful, having a paradigm with organizing principles can significantly improve the chances of our obtaining intended results. Use of the six basic principles of the IMPACT Paradigm can facilitate the process of engaging others and intentionally causing predetermined effects in their behaviors and cognitions.

We see how all the paradigm principles are related to one another. They work together to ensure highly effective, engaging, and dynamic communication interactions. We can hardly use one without using all the others.

The more I teach and coach professionals to communicate with impact, the more I realize the importance of understanding and deliberately practicing the essential elements of the paradigm. It is easy to believe that people are either naturally strong or weak communicators and will remain that way, but by applying the six principles unified in the IMPACT Paradigm, we can all take our communication effectiveness to the next level—no matter where we are at present. The rest of the book shows how to do this.

2

THE IMPACT PARADIGM—
WHY IT WORKS

Success, for many of us, depends on our ability to communicate effectively and achieve results working with, and through, people. The IMPACT Paradigm facilitates our success. This chapter focuses on why the paradigm works. It underscores how we, as strategic communicators, benefit from applying the paradigm principles—answering the central question: "What's in it for us?"

First, we look at how the IMPACT Paradigm provides us with a framework of ideas, guides our actions, and supports a beneficial way of thinking about communication interactions. Then, we discuss how it benefits us to have a simple, whole, and practical framework that is easy to remember, easy to use, and applicable across communication situations.

The IMPACT Paradigm Provides a Framework of Ideas

This paradigm organizes a framework of ideas about strategic communication. The conceptual framework promotes our understanding of the general viewpoints, beliefs, assumptions, and practices involved in communicating to achieve goals and outcomes.

Thomas Kuhn's influential book *The Structure of Scientific Revolutions* is often cited when paradigms in any field of study are discussed. He looked at a paradigm in two ways: as an exemplar—either an exemplary model or an exemplary practice; and as a recognized group of assumptions, concepts, methods, problems, and theories. As a philosopher of science, Kuhn wrote about paradigms as "the practices that define a scientific discipline at a certain point in time" (1962, 10). Essentially, a paradigm is a framework that contains all the views about a subject and gives us a way to look at that subject.

We can use the IMPACT Paradigm to look at, think about, and analyze how the principles and practices of strategic communication relate to the larger purpose of achieving intended results. Having this organizing framework builds our understanding of how the complex process of strategic communication works.

The IMPACT Paradigm Guides Actions

The paradigm principles guide our actions and help us to navigate the process of communicating purposefully by clarifying complexities.

"A paradigm is a worldview, a general perspective, a way of breaking down the complexity of the real world" (Patton 1990, 37). It focuses attention on the fundamental aspects of the process so we can make informed decisions and think about our courses of actions.

Use of the IMPACT Paradigm enables us to gain insights about the actions we take in the beginning, middle, and end of communication interactions. Not only does the paradigm help us to deconstruct the process and plan our actions, it also increases our understanding of where, when, and how to make course corrections along the way.

The IMPACT Paradigm Supports a Way of Thinking

The IMPACT Paradigm supports a beneficial way of thinking about our communication interactions. It facilitates an impact mindset.

We all have mindsets, defined in the dictionary as "a particular way of thinking: a person's attitude or set of opinions about something." The mindset we have in a particular field of activity guides us in that field of activity. The importance of mindsets cannot be overstated because "*the view you adopt for yourself* profoundly affects the way you lead your life" (Dweck 2006, 6). Two examples follow.

Chris Argyris, Harvard University management scholar, discussed mindsets in an interview published in the HBS series *Working Knowledge*:

> There are two dominant mindsets in the world of business or any kind of organization. One is a productive mindset, and it says it's a good idea to seek valid knowledge, it's a good idea to craft your conversations so you make explicit what you are thinking and trying to examine . . . Then there's another mindset I call the defensive mindset. The idea is that even if you are seeking valid knowledge, you are seeking only that kind of valid knowledge that protects yourself or your organization or your department—it is defensive.
>
> (Stark 2004)

Argyris developed a way to move from the defensive to the productive mindset through a process that he calls double loop learning. This process brings into congruence the values people believe their actions are based on ("espoused theory") and the values implied by their actions ("theory-in-use"). Mindsets are powerful. They develop over time but they can be changed.

Carol Dweck, Stanford University psychologist known for her research on student motivation, wrote in her book *Mindset: The New Psychology of Success*:

> The growth mindset is based on the belief that your basic qualities are things you can cultivate through your efforts. Although people may differ in every which way—in their initial talents and aptitudes, interests, or temperaments— everyone can change and grow through application and experience.
>
> (2006, 7)

She differentiated this growth mindset from a fixed mindset that is based on "believing that your qualities are carved in stone" (2006, 6). She stated that, "Just by knowing about the two mindsets, you can start thinking and reacting in new ways" (2006, 46). Dweck's research and the research of others in multiple fields of study have proven that keeping a particular mindset in our thoughts significantly affects how we engage in an area of activity.

Adopting an impact mindset enables us to examine our actions, consider unresolved problems, and recognize the ways we are approaching our communication to achieve desired results. It also encourages us to try out new behaviors and then reflect on them, which is critical to becoming a more effective communicator.

The IMPACT Paradigm is Simple, not Simplistic

Strategic communicators benefit from using the IMPACT Paradigm because it is simple. "Everything should be made as simple as possible, but not simpler" (Albert Einstein).

Most likely, this statement is a simplified version, perhaps an editor's paraphrase, of the following quote from "On the Method of Theoretical Physics," a Herbert Spence Lecture, Oxford (June 10, 1933), published in *Philosophy of Science*, Volume 1, No. 2 (April 1934), pages 163–169: "It can scarcely be denied that the supreme goal of all theory is to make the irreducible basic elements as simple and as few as possible without having to surrender the adequate representation of a single datum of experience" (Einstein 1934, 165).

Often seen in books and heard in speeches, the simplified version uses the KISS principle (an acronym for "keep it short and simple" or "keep it short and straightforward"). This makes the statement clear, memorable, and useful. It includes only what is essential, of central importance.

Similarly, the IMPACT Paradigm is simple so we can easily understand it, remember it, and use it. As we said, it is simple but not simplistic. The paradigm emerged from embracing the complexities of the communication process, and then honing in on the essential elements. It focuses on what matters most. It is streamlined, stripped of non-essentials, and organized.

The simple nature of the paradigm allows us to focus on essential communication principles that are interrelated, effectively integrated, and combine together to form an organized whole.

The IMPACT Paradigm is a Whole System

The IMPACT Paradigm, one complete whole of interrelated components, enables us to understand the communication process by first looking at its basic components and then seeing it as a whole. It recognizes that optimizing one part and not the others can have an adverse effect on both the communication process and its outcomes. It embraces holism by considering how the parts form a whole and ensuring that the parts work together well to serve the strategic purpose of communication.

Ludwig von Bertalanffy, biologist and systems theorist, wrote:

> The central position of the concept of wholeness in biology, psychology, sociology and other sciences is generally acknowledged. What is meant by this concept is indicated by expressions such as "system," "gestalt," "organism," "interaction," "the whole is more than the sum of its parts" and the like . . . General System Theory is a new scientific doctrine of "wholeness."
>
> (1950, 142)

He promoted systems thinking to aid in understanding the interacting elements of any complex whole.

Just as the IMPACT Paradigm is informed by holism, each component of the paradigm is also informed by holism. Consider how a holistic perspective is embodied in each principle.

Intending: When we engage in the purposeful action of intending, our brain and body work together. We use a holistic process of thinking about what we want as a result of a communication and directing our actions toward attaining that outcome. Our awareness of the importance of intending, thinking and acting purposefully, significantly affects how we approach our communication interactions.

Messaging: As we convey our thoughts and feelings, we use multiple modes of expression. Our messages—verbal and non-verbal, directly expressed and indirectly implied—are formed from our words, body language, and vocal expressions. The principle of messaging directly relates to holism. The individual parts of our expression interact with each other and combine into complete and congruous messages.

Presence: We are living systems, composed of component parts that function as a whole. Networks of communication exist between our body and brain. "While the nervous system uses neurotransmitters as its chemical signals, the endocrine system uses hormones" (Society for Neuroscience 2012). These important messages within the brain and between the body and brain affect how we show up physically and vocally in any given moment. What happens to one part of us affects the other parts. A holistic view of presence focuses on these crucial interactions, recognizing the highly complex interrelationship between our body and mind.

Attending: Attending can be thought of as meeting. When one living system meets with another living system, it creates a whole new system that is more than (or to be precise, *other* than) the sum of its parts. Attending establishes a relational connection, facilitates co-participation, and sets the conditions for creating shared meaning. This is a holistic view of the principle of attending.

Connecting: Maintaining a relational connection is necessary for ensuring co-participation in communication interactions. Connecting places importance on the dynamic between the people who are interacting. When we focus on the connection between speaker and listener, we are using a holistic approach to engaging in communication interactions and improving our communication effectiveness.

Together: Conversations facilitate the process of meaning making and agreeing on goals and action. In conversation, we construct, exchange, and share meaning. We think together, learn together, and reflect together. We also create the conditions for agreeing on and coordinating our actions through conversations. The principle of conversing together to make meaning, to cooperate, and to collaborate comes from a perspective that is holistic.

The IMPACT Paradigm is Easy to Understand

Focusing on one whole leads to clarity. The IMPACT Paradigm is a single organizing framework that makes it easy to understand the whole process of communicating purposefully. Using one framework enables us to understand how to approach our communication activities in a comprehensive way.

Looking at how two parts work together creates greater clarity of the whole. As we identified in the first chapter, there are two sets of paradigm principles. The first set (intending, messaging, and presence) focuses on expression and what you want to achieve as a result of your communication. The second set (attending, connecting, together) focuses on interactions with others. Together, these two sets make it easy to understand how adjustments made to any of the interacting parts affect the process of communication and its outcomes.

Creating a pattern of three is often referred to as the "power of three." Putting three elements together to create a pattern is used effectively in both writing and speaking. The IMPACT Paradigm has three principles that can be thought of as intrapersonal ("occurring within the self") and three principles that are interpersonal ("occurring between persons"). The principles of intending, messaging, and presence can be considered intrapersonal because they relate primarily to the actions and communication behaviors of one person. The principles of attending, connecting, and together are primarily interpersonal because they involve two or more people engaged in communication interactions.

Having one whole and two sets of three principles increases clarity, simplifies complexity, and makes the IMPACT Paradigm both easy to understand and easy to remember.

The IMPACT Paradigm is Easy to Remember

IMPACT is a mnemonic for remembering what I consider to be the six most important aspects of purposeful communication.

- **I**ntending
- **M**essaging
- **P**resence
- **A**ttending
- **C**onnecting
- **T**ogether

Using the IMPACT mnemonic makes it easy for us to remember the interconnected parts of the whole—the six communication principles. It helps us to have ready access to the simple, whole, and practical IMPACT Paradigm, and thus facilitates our purposeful use of communication activities to achieve goals and outcomes.

Based on my extensive experience in communication, these are the six main areas where people struggle the most. They are also the areas where I've seen people significantly improve their communication by making only small adjustments. The six components of the paradigm integrate what is most critical for becoming better, more effective strategic communicators.

The IMPACT Paradigm is Applicable across Communication Situations

As a paradigm, all the interrelated principles can be applied anytime, anywhere, and by anyone during their communication interactions at work.

Consider a typical day at work. It may involve leading or participating in one-on-one meetings and small or large group meetings. It may involve presenting new ideas or updates to individuals and groups. It may involve negotiating with one or more people. In banks, law firms, hospitals, universities, start-up tech companies, and other professional environments, we communicate in a range of different situations.

The IMPACT Paradigm can be applied to any communication situation at work. It is equally applicable to our interactions with one person and groups of any size. We use essentially the same principles and practices to achieve desired outcomes in one-on-one, small group and large group interactions.

People at all levels of experience—from graduate students to faculty, from new hires to seasoned professionals—can use the paradigm principles. In addition, we can continually learn about the effectiveness of these communication principles when we observe others using them during their interactions.

The next chapter will focus on specific examples of work-related interactions to illustrate the applicability of the IMPACT Paradigm in a variety of different communication situations.

Conclusion

Throughout this chapter, I have highlighted the practical nature and benefits of using the IMPACT Paradigm. Not only does the paradigm provide us with one complete organized framework to help us understand the process of communicating to achieve outcomes, it also simplifies its complexities and helps guide our actions. Importantly, this paradigm keeps us focused on having the kind of impact we want to have when we use communication in a purposeful way.

One of the most salient benefits of the IMPACT Paradigm is that it can be applied across communication situations. Our communication interactions at work provide us with many opportunities to engage with others to achieve our outcomes, reflect on our actions, and recognize ways to improve our effectiveness.

As a teacher, coach, and student of expert performance, I've come to understand the indispensable importance of having an impact mindset, being aware of our communication actions, and practicing to continually improve our communication effectiveness. I value what K. Anders Ericsson calls deliberate practice, "effortful activities designed to optimize performance" (Ericsson, Krampe and Tesch-Romer 1993, 363). To facilitate practice, I limited the number of paradigm components, use the IMPACT mnemonic to make them memorable, and provide exercises for focused practice of skills related to each component later in the book. Our ability to make small changes in one aspect of our communication can result in big changes for our overall effectiveness.

The two chapters that follow show how individuals met actual communication challenges by applying the IMPACT Paradigm to a range of situations, and how we can use the framework to overcome some of the most common communication concerns.

PART TWO

Strategic Communication in Action

3

COMMUNICATION SITUATIONS

Over the years, I've listened to thousands of students and hundreds of clients in a range of professions tell me that they are comfortable engaging in some types of communication interactions and uncomfortable engaging in others.

At first, I explained to them that the same principles apply equally to one-on-one, small group and large group communication interactions; that the principles are common to all purposeful communication. Now, I am going beyond this. My primary reason for writing *Strategic Communication at Work: The IMPACT Paradigm* is to empower readers to achieve intended outcomes with high impact in all types of communication situations.

Which types of communication interactions do you have now or expect to have in the future? Consider the following list and then reflect on others that are not on this list:

- Client Meetings
- Staff Meetings
- Networking
- Team Presentations

- Board Meeting Presentations
- Academic Presentations
- Project Updates
- Negotiations
- Workplace Conversations
- Job Interviews
- Media Appearances
- Training
- Counseling
- Mentoring
- Selling Products or Services
- Investor Pitches
- Client Pitches
- Client Reviews
- Keynote Speeches
- Teaching

In this chapter, I describe nine communication situations. These specific interactions were relayed to me by people (fictional names are used to preserve their confidentiality) with whom I've worked over my years of teaching and coaching. Each one-on-one, small group and large group situation shows the IMPACT Paradigm principles in practice. These communication interactions include: 1—a workplace conversation; 2—a corporate pitch; 3—a presentation; 4—a meeting; 5—a project update; 6—a negotiation; 7—networking; 8—a job interview; and 9—a keynote speech.

In Part One, we discussed the importance of starting with the end in mind. The two situations that follow highlight the principle of intending and illustrate other IMPACT Paradigm principles at work. One is a workplace conversation between an employee and her superior in a financial services firm and the other is a pitch for funds by a team leader in a luxury goods company. In both situations, the communicators started with the end in mind and achieved results that exceeded their desired outcomes.

Situation 1: A Workplace Conversation— Managing Up

How do you initiate a difficult conversation with a superior without putting your job at risk? How do you successfully achieve your desired outcome and at the same time, strengthen your working relationship? Jenna began with intending—the first IMPACT Paradigm principle.

It took a year for Jenna, a 28-year old Assistant Vice President working in the compliance department of an investment bank, to have the courage to initiate a difficult workplace conversation with her boss, Dave, the Director of the department.

They worked together in local government for two years. Then Dave recruited Jenna to work in his group at an investment bank because he valued her intelligence and work ethic. They had a great rapport. For six years, Dave was a supportive mentor to Jenna. She enthusiastically took on all the additional responsibilities he gave her, displaying a strong personal commitment to successfully complete all of her projects.

Then came a serious recession.

The bank was undergoing a tremendous amount of scrutiny and this was having a major impact on the compliance group. People were getting laid off. Those who remained in the group were inundated with reports to comply with regulations.

Intending for a Change

Under enormous stress, Dave asked Jenna to take on another responsibility. Besides writing her own investigative reports, Dave wanted her to review and make all necessary corrections to the compliance reports generated by the other four team members. He knew Jenna was conscientious and could handle a heavy workload.

No title change, recognition, or raise came with this added responsibility.

For a full year, Jenna worked long hours every day to handle her increased workload. She felt she owed Dave a lot, including her loyalty. Jenna was committed to showing him by her actions that she was grateful for the opportunities given to her, including her recent promotion and the company's financial support of her MBA studies.

Struggling to complete all her job responsibilities and growing more distressed each day, she eventually had to acknowledge that the situation was unsustainable. It was not possible for her to be effective with the added responsibility of being the review intermediary for all reports generated by the team. Jenna needed to address this situation with Dave.

Broaching a difficult subject with him was something she had never done before. In the past, their communication interactions were about everyday tasks or simply small talk. But now she had to stand up for herself and assert her opinion in conversation with Dave, even though it could have negatively affected their working relationship.

The only thing Jenna did to prepare for this conversation was focus on her intent—to get approval from Dave to relinquish her responsibility for making the revisions on every compliance report generated by the team. She knew it would be critical to stick to her intent throughout the conversation to keep it on course and achieve her desired outcome.

Mustering up her courage, Jenna decided to initiate the conversation with Dave mid-week, rather than at the end of the week when all the reports were due. She waited until most people had left work to have an end-of-day conversation with him.

Jenna got out of her cubicle, stood outside the glass walls of Dave's office, and then knocked on his door.

Messaging in a New Way

"Do you have a moment to talk with me?" Judging by the surprised expression on Dave's face, Jenna knew she had gotten his attention.

Hearing the tone of her voice and seeing the serious expression on her face, he said, "Oh my. What's wrong?" She responded, "Nothing. I'd like to air some ideas with you and bring up some things that are on my mind." "Of course. Come in," said Dave.

Jenna took a seat next to him.

Setting the precedent that she wasn't always going to be the bubbly, enthusiastic person who would take on any responsibility with a smiling face, Jenna deliberately spoke slowly and clearly to add gravitas to her messaging. She chose her words carefully to explain the situation, starting with some positive comments.

"I'm grateful for the opportunities I've been given—taking on investigative work, developing new policies and procedures, and leading some meetings. I like contributing." Dave responded, "Of course, but obviously you're not here to talk about this."

Then she spoke directly about the issue, "I'm fine with doing all these things, but I cannot do them effectively with the added responsibility of a second review of the reports."

Jenna felt totally justified in making her request because of her certainty that the current work situation was unsustainable.

Attending to Each Other, Connecting on Current Concerns

Dave rubbed his head, a behavior Jenna had seen him exhibit when he felt stressed. Then he explained, "I only asked you to do this because I am getting so many more reports and I don't have the time to look over all of them." Although Dave had never explicitly told her he was feeling stressed and overwhelmed by what was happening at the bank, he began to do so.

Not only was this the first time Jenna brought up something difficult to Dave, it also was the first time he had shared with her something difficult that was going on for him.

Jenna deliberately maintained an outward focus throughout their conversation so she could see his movements and facial expressions, and know when it was appropriate to ask questions or respond with comments. By visually attending and actively listening to him, she was able to direct the conversation toward the overall situation at the bank. She asked him where he thought the team was going in light of all the changes, and how the team could function in the future.

They shared how they approach their work, how they see themselves, and how they handle their workflow. They also talked about expectations and the challenges of team management.

The connection Jenna established by attending to Dave remained strong throughout. Their conversation flowed naturally and easily from her experience since the fallout of the financial crisis to his experience, and then to their shared experience.

This mutual sharing allowed Jenna to gain clarity and better appreciate the situation from Dave's perspective. She understood that Dave gave her the added responsibility because he trusted her and did not have the time to do it himself. But neither did Jenna.

Time was the issue that needed to be addressed.

Together, Confronting the Future

Jenna directed the conversation to finding a solution to the workload problem moving forward, "Given this, let's go back to what we were talking about before." She suggested something that occurred to her on the spot, "Here is what I can do. Once you look over the reports and tell me which ones seem problematic, I can sit down with the team members who wrote those reports and train them on how it should be done."

She offered to create a template to give to the other four team members so they could do their own revisions. Then, when reports went to Dave, they would be ready for his final approval. Jenna's plan enabled the other members of the team to fix their reports, alleviating the need for an intermediary. This was a much more efficient approach. Dave agreed with Jenna.

Together, they reached a mutually satisfactory agreement. Jenna felt a tremendous weight lifted off her shoulders, and expressed her appreciation for being relieved of the additional review responsibility.

As a result of this conversation, Jenna strengthened the relationship with her boss, increased their level of trust with one another, opened their communication, and achieved her intended outcome.

Engaging in this workplace conversation was a profound and transformative experience for Jenna. She learned that she had the courage to speak up and advocate for herself. From then on, Jenna was able to engage in open communication with her boss. She recognized that when a problem arose in the future, she wouldn't necessarily have to fix it herself. Instead, she could talk with him about it.

Subsequently, there was another round of layoffs at the bank. Jenna knew she could go to her boss and ask him what was happening.

Situation 2: A Corporate Pitch—Requesting $1,000,000

Competition was stiff. Many teams in the business unit of a leading luxury goods company were vying for the same funds. All of their proposals were to be pitched to the President and her Chief Financial Officer (CFO) in the same week.

Aware that there was a negative perception of their business unit in the current environment, the corporate affairs team was preparing to make a pitch to secure one million dollars to support a reputation campaign for the unit. By making a pitch in which the return on investment would be more qualitative than quantitative, the team was taking a big chance.

This would not be the kind of pitch that the President and CFO were used to hearing.

Joni, the team leader, carefully considered how the orientations of the President of the business unit and the CFO might differ. Most likely, the President would be more oriented towards the importance of changing public perception and more willing to make an investment in an area where it is difficult to quantify the return on investment. The CFO would likely view the team's investment case as an "uncharacteristic spend" and would want to know what the investment would look like, as well as see some measurable return on investment.

Intending for Proposal Approval

On Monday morning, Joni learned about the opportunity to make a pitch. She met with her corporate affairs team in a conference room for a brainstorming session and they created their proposal that afternoon. Joni scheduled the pitch meeting for the next day because she wanted to get her team's proposal in as early in the week as possible.

They had a clear intended outcome: to get approval for the funds needed for their reputation campaign by the end of the week.

It was out of the norm to invest in reputation building on a business unit level, rather than on a corporate level. For this reason, Joni's team thought it was unrealistic to expect to get approval right away for one million dollars. Instead, they aimed to build some positive momentum for an affirmative answer by the end of the week.

On Tuesday, Joni and her communications counterpart met with the President of their global business unit and her close working partner, the CFO, to pitch the team's proposal. They sat at a conference table in the office of the President. Joni handed them her team's carefully structured proposal deck. She had not given it to them in advance because she wanted to control the narrative and present a compelling investment case in person.

The first section set the context, creating the need for supporting the proposal. It had numerous press clippings illustrating the current situation. It included clippings about some recent activities showing the progress their business unit had made. Whereas several years earlier the business unit wasn't viewed as a relevant player, now they were relevant in the product category but seen in a negative light.

The second section described the three initiatives and the stakeholder groups that would be reached by each one.

It specified how each initiative would overcome obstacles and lead to a more favorable reputation, as well as specific qualitative and quantitative metrics, such as favorable mentions, speaking engagements, and media impression numbers.

The third and final section detailed the fund allocation for each initiative, along with specific next steps for implementation.

Not surprisingly, the CFO started flipping to the back pages to see the budget numbers as soon as Joni handed out the decks. In a friendly and diplomatic way, Joni said, "If we can focus on the context first, it's going to help frame what we think the need is and then from there, we will look at resources." This worked well because from that point until the end, everyone in the room focused on the same content.

To tell the story in a way that would ensure achieving the intended outcome required setting the context, creating the need upfront, and maintaining the three-part structure.

Messaging with Purpose

The pitch lasted about 30 minutes. Joni deliberately spoke in short sentences because she knew the President and CFO were very busy people who valued concision and precision.

With a tone of authority, she laid out three initiatives for engaging with the public in a new way. These were a global media tour that included round table discussions and hands-on experiences with their products for news reporters; sponsorship of speaking engagements for the head of the business unit at conferences attended by key innovation and environmental influencers; and a new internal campaign to orient colleagues towards a particular narrative about the brand essence of their business unit.

She paused periodically to ask if the President or CFO had questions or needed clarification. Joni wanted to make sure she cleared up any bias or possible misunderstanding about any of her numbers before moving ahead to the next point. They asked some questions, such as "what would this look like?" and "should another company split the cost?"

When Joni and her colleague heard multiple questions that started with the word "when," this was a positive sign. It led them to believe there was a good chance they would get the funding for their proposal, or at least the funds for that particular piece of it.

To demonstrate confidence and conviction in her verbal messaging and to gain the trust of the President and CFO that the investment would achieve the outcome she was telling them it would, Joni maintained eye contact. This also enabled her to keep a close watch on their physical reactions. About half-way through the pitch, Joni noticed that the President sat back in her chair, getting physically comfortable. She looked relaxed while attentively listening. This was another positive sign.

Joni was purposeful about her non-verbal messaging. She oriented her upper body to directly face whoever was speaking. She deliberately rested her elbows and forearms on the table so she could freely gesture to reinforce her words and feelings. She allowed herself to use facial expressions to convey understanding and empathy for the comments made by the President and CFO about the initiatives.

Sitting up straight on the edge of her chair, close to the table, Joni remained alert. Her presence was strong throughout the pitch.

Joni knew the proposal so well that she was able to stay focused on her desired outcome, while paying attention to the behavior of people in the room. She was able to communicate the passion and excitement of the team to do the work on behalf of the business unit, while engaging the President and CFO throughout the pitch.

Being present—mind and body—throughout the pitch clearly had an impact.

Together, Taking Action

"Listen. We really need to do this. Go for it," was the President's response. Then she turned to her partner, the CFO, and said "We can make this work." He affirmed that they could with a one-word answer, "Yes." The President and CFO agreed that this reputation campaign should be supported with an investment of one million dollars.

After expressing their thanks for being allowed to make this unconventional pitch, the President acknowledged Joni and her colleague for setting the context in the beginning of their pitch to help her and the CFO understand the need for the initiative and how this investment would address it. Joni was very pleased to know that the strategic messaging choices her team had made helped them to achieve, and even to exceed, their desired outcome.

Although calm in the meeting, Joni and her colleague excitedly gave each other high fives as soon as they left the President's office. They were thrilled that the corporate affairs team received immediate approval for the funds needed for their reputation campaign.

Year two, they did it again and got another million dollars.

In Part One, we examined congruous messaging, a vital principle that maximizes impact when communicating with others. The next two situations highlight the principle of messaging. One is a presentation by the general counsel at the annual meeting of a homebuilding company, and the other is a small group meeting of doctors at a hospital. Each communication interaction had a completely different tone—one playful, one serious—but both required congruous messaging. The general counsel and the Chief of Staff at the hospital applied the other IMPACT Paradigm principles, as well.

Situation 3: A Presentation—Wry Smiles at the Annual Meeting

The legal counsel was preparing his presentation for the company's annual meeting. How could he make his message memorable?

Alex had a dual role at the homebuilding company of 300 employees—legal counsel for the company and leader of its affiliated title company that conducts real estate settlements. He was aware that the title company was underappreciated by the rest of the company. In fact, the seven homebuilding divisions of the company often forgot that the title company was even a part of the business. It was not surprising to Alex that the title company employees sometimes felt frustrated and neglected.

He wanted to do something to remedy this situation in his upcoming presentation at the company's annual meeting. A naturally introverted person, more a listener than a talker, Alex welcomed this opportunity to get everyone who worked at the homebuilding company to appreciate the title company's contribution, and to recognize its employees as significant players.

Messaging to Engage the Audience

First, he considered what the company employees would expect from the upcoming annual meeting.

Most likely, the leader of each of the seven homebuilding divisions would deliver a slide presentation standing behind the podium in a ballroom at a large conference center in a hotel.

Each presentation would consist of an update on the prior year's results and the division's goals for the coming year. After the presentations about the seven homebuilding divisions, there would be a short presentation about the affiliated title company delivered by Alex, the general counsel. Lunch would then be served, followed by an awards ceremony.

Next, he decided that he needed to do or say something unexpected in his annual meeting presentation to change the company employees' perception of the title company.

Alex considered various messaging strategies he learned from his legal training and work experience. From the oral presentations he delivered in moot court competitions, he learned to convey emphasis with his voice by slowing down, raising his volume, or pausing after each important point. From his work experience as a teacher, he learned many ways to use his words, actions, and vocal delivery to energize the students and to hold their attention.

These past experiences informed the approach Alex would take with his annual meeting presentation—high energy, surprise, playfulness, and a great deal of vocal variety. To grab the audience's attention from the start, Alex would begin his presentation in a playful way. He would ask the group a question that he was quite certain they would not be able to answer easily.

At the February annual meeting, all of the employees from the corporate office and the six remote locations of the homebuilding company were seated in a large ballroom. When it was Alex's turn to make his presentation about the title company, he went to the podium, picked up the detachable microphone, and walked toward the audience to engage them in a direct conversation. Everyone stopped talking, fidgeting, and looking at their phones. The audience was completely silent, waiting to see what would happen next.

Alex held up a $50 gift card and asked for volunteers who could name the eight profit centers of the homebuilding company. Members of the audience raised their hands. They were enthusiastic about identifying all of the company's profit centers, but couldn't. They were stumped on the last one.

Walking toward each person who attempted to answer the question, he could feel the excitement in the room about answering the question. He called on several more individuals. One after another, everyone who volunteered to answer the question could only name the seven homebuilding divisions.

Attending to the Audience Responses

The audience was entertained and having fun, as was Alex. He saw wry smiles on the face of his boss and one of his direct reports who knew what he was doing. In addition, they both knew there was a dead giveaway in the annual meeting agenda that every attendee had received—the title company was listed there.

At one point, Alex felt a bit of tension in the room. There were some moments of silence. Alex let the silence happen.

After allowing the audience to struggle a bit more with this tricky question, he called on the payroll processor of the whole company who had her hand raised. At first, even she struggled with naming all of the company's profit centers. Eventually, she came up with the title company as the eighth profit center and received the gift card.

Everyone was off their phones, looking up, listening, and paying attention. Once Alex saw that the audience's interest and attention was focused on the title company, he proceeded to present the important facts about the business of the company. He told them how much money the title company made last year, and its plans for the coming year. Alex wanted the meeting attendees to know that the title company had grown every year. Giving them a projected budget that showed growth made an impact on the company's employees. They realized that the affiliated title company compared favorably with the smallest of the homebuilding divisions and was almost as big.

Intending for Company-Wide Recognition

The presentation had a good result. It got people thinking about the affiliated title company.

Alex delivered a memorable presentation and was effective in achieving his intended outcome: to call attention to the existence and contribution of the title company and increase appreciation for the work of its employees.

Without using notes or slides, he successfully accomplished this by first grabbing the audience's attention with a surprising, entertaining, light-hearted opening. Once he had their attention, he kept their interest with his congruous messaging and high-energy delivery throughout the presentation.

Before Alex's presentation, the company employees gave no thought to the affiliated title company. After his presentation, people were finally recognizing and talking about the contribution of the title company.

Situation 4: A Small Group Meeting—Revoke or Resign Hospital Privileges

The performance and behavior problems of Dr. Farr, an anesthesiologist at Farmington Community Hospital, continued for over a year.

The first problem was this physician's sloppiness in the documentation of the medical record. This had an impact on the hospital's ratings and Medicare scores. Medicare was looking for a number of specific SCIP (Surgical Care Improvement Project) measures. One measure was the anesthesia record, where the time and the type of anesthesia given had to be documented. For over a year, Dr. Farr had been extremely sloppy and careless about his documentation.

The second major problem was related to cleanliness and safety. He repeatedly failed to throw away needles and syringes in the appropriate disposal containers. Dr. Farr would leave the area where he was attending to a patient and at the end of the case, walk away leaving hazardous material that was dangerous to the staff.

Each time the previous Chairman of Anesthesia had a conversation with Dr. Farr about his performance and behavior problems, he said he would do better but never did.

When the new Chairman of Anesthesia recognized these problems, he was outraged that a member of his department couldn't meet basic behavioral standards. He spoke to this physician on a number of occasions, gave him warnings but got nowhere.

Dr. Farr would improve for a week and then fall back into the same problematic behavior.

Messaging a Forced Choice

Chief of Staff Dr. Mackay, who had oversight of the medical, surgery, and anesthesia department chairs, needed to meet with Dr. Farr to resolve the situation once and for all.

Dr. Mackay organized a pre-meeting with two other physician leaders, the Chief Medical Officer and the Chairman of Anesthesia, to discuss the problem. The Chief Medical Officer had worked closely with Dr. Mackay for many years at the hospital, and the Chairman of Anesthesia was Dr. Farr's direct supervisor.

After about ten minutes, the three physician leaders reached consensus. They wanted Dr. Farr to improve his behavior but were skeptical that he would. They talked about possibly limiting or revoking his hospital privileges. If they were to revoke his privileges, it would have serious consequences for Dr. Farr's career. It also would involve a difficult and lengthy administrative process.

The meeting with Dr. Farr and the Chief of Staff, the Chief Medical Officer, and the Chairman of Anesthesia took place in the office of the Chief Medical Officer.

"We're here to talk about your performance. There are two issues: documentation and the needle problem. I've spoken to you about these issues many times. We're not getting anywhere," stated the Chairman of Anesthesia.

Dr. Farr rattled off a list of excuses, "Well, you know, sometimes I see what other people do and they're sloppier than I am, and their records aren't always perfect, and in an emergency case, it isn't always easy to remember to write things down, and . . ." He denied that he was any different than anyone else.

Clearly, Dr. Farr was not responding to the statement of facts with an acknowledgement of his behavior and a commitment to change.

That's when Chief of Staff Dr. Mackay came in as the heavyweight. His words and voice underscored the gravity of the situation.

"Look, Dr. Farr, you may be in many respects a safe technical anesthesiologist. But, what you are saying about your behavior, vis a vis other anesthesiologists, is just not true. Occasionally, someone has these sorts of problems but you're a repeat offender. You're an outlier. This is not new. Your previous department chair couldn't get you to comply. I know other people have talked to you about this. The current chairman is talking to you, and now you're denying it."

Then Dr. Mackay presented him with a forced choice. "We can take this a couple of ways. We can take formal action against your privileges. We can revoke your privileges. The other way we can go with this is you can just resign your privileges now. And it's probably best for you to resign your privileges now."

Unwavering in his resolve to address these problems for the last time, Dr. Mackay continued speaking in a low, slow, quiet voice. "If we revoke your privileges, then that will be a permanent red flag on your record. You're not going to be able to get a job in any other hospital where you would want to work, and we don't think that's a good outcome for you. We also don't believe you can comply because you haven't demonstrated that. So we think the better thing for you to do would be to resign your privileges now."

Dr. Farr did not want to resign. He also did not want his hospital privileges revoked.

Attending to a Doctor in Distress

Chief of Staff Dr. Mackay leaned forward in his chair and never took his eyes off of the physician. By attending to the changes in Dr. Farr's posture, muscular tension, and body movements throughout the meeting, he knew he was having an impact.

Facing two undesirable options, the physician was physically twitching, sitting back in his chair with clenched fists.

"No. I can do better. This is not going to be a problem going forward. I don't want to resign. I'm not going to resign. I'll do anything that I have to do," protested Dr. Farr.

As he spoke up for himself and presented a new, more favorable option, he sat up straighter, became less stiff, and the twitchy body movements stopped.

"I'll do whatever I have to do." Hearing this, the look on Dr. Mackay's face conveyed the skepticism of all the physician leaders. Without speaking, his expression said "Really?"

The Chief Medical Officer responded, "If you're going to continue, then you will have to have absolute compliance. There's no room for variance here."

Dr. Farr professed that there would be absolute compliance and he would work out the details with the Chairman of Anesthesia.

Together, Agreeing on a New Option

The upshot of the meeting was an agreement to let the physician take the new, more favorable option and work out specific action steps with the Chairman of Anesthesia.

They decided together that Dr. Farr would continue in his position and meet monthly with the Chairman of Anesthesia. Each month, the Chairman would report on Dr. Farr's performance using the Focused Professional Practice Evaluation process. For six months, every single one of Dr. Farr's anesthesia records would be audited.

The outcome was far better than anyone expected. The performance and behavior problems stopped entirely. The physician kept his word and kept his job.

Months later, Dr. Mackay noticed that Dr. Farr averted making eye contact with him whenever their paths crossed in the hospital. When it was apparent that Dr. Farr was performing consistently well, Dr. Mackay took him aside and said, "I just want you to know that I'm really happy you were able to turn this around. I'm delighted that you're here and able to perform like this."

You read in Part One about presence. The next two interactions illustrate the principle of presence, as well as other IMPACT

Paradigm principles. When a young management consultant delivered a project update to an important client, it was essential for her to be fully focused on all fronts. When a trained musician attending business school used a thorough preparation process, she was able to be fully present at her job interviews and to secure an offer for the marketing position she wanted at a consumer products company.

Situation 5: A Project Update—High Stakes for a Consultant

The future of a major project was at stake.

The management consulting firm's most important client was hesitant to continue to the next phase of a management and leadership training program for the top 200 leaders of their global organization. The client, a privately held financial services firm, wanted to review the progress made by the participants before moving forward. The seven key client leads from this firm would decide based on the report prepared by a young consultant named Francesca.

Participant surveys were handed out to collect data for evaluating the training, but unfortunately, the numbers did not look good. The data was in the 70th percentile for the various satisfaction metrics but the goal was to be in the 85th percentile. This was troubling to Francesca and her team of four co-consultants.

How could they convey the true impact of the training session with the current quantitative data?

Presence, Harnessing the Power to Meet the Challenge

The next update meeting would be critically important. Francesca had to do a great deal of work on this satisfaction issue in advance so she could be fully present when she gave her progress report to the client leads.

She and her team members dug into the survey data. They found that despite what the quantitative metrics said, the qualitative comments made by the survey respondents underscored the impact of the training session. As an example, one respondent wrote,

> I was struggling with one of my team members who was bringing the whole team down. I didn't know how to redirect him. We had many difficult conversations that had gone poorly, but because of the exercise that we did in the training, I now know how I'm going to move this person forward.

The team of consultants did two things with the qualitative data.

First, they quantified the qualitative data. They noted how many times each type of positive qualitative comment came up so they could create metrics for the qualitative data. This was important because their financial services client was quantitatively driven.

Second, they selected comments made by the most highly respected individuals within the organization. The consultants had learned from previous remarks made by their client that they were driven not only by numbers, but also by whether an individual was highly regarded in the organization. For that reason, they pulled out illuminating comments from key people to highlight and bring to life each type of positive qualitative comment.

Then Francesca and the other consultants did a third and final thing. To better understand why the scores were low, they dug further into the data and realized the two quantitative questions on the survey were framed in ways that skewed the data.

One quantitative question asked participants to rate the value for time spent. Because the training participants felt that a four-hour session was too long, they gave a low rating to the value for time spent. The consultants came to understand that there was no issue with the value of the training session, rather the issue was the length of the session.

The other quantitative question on the survey asked participants how likely they were to recommend this training session to a colleague. Because they valued saving people's time so much, they were not likely to recommend it to a colleague. The consultants realized the participants did not have an issue with the impact of the training, but rather they felt the session would take up too much of their colleagues' time.

With these findings, Francesca had the evidence she needed to get client approval and a specific date for the next training session. After rehearsing over and over, she was finally ready to show up fully present at the update meeting. Feeling well-prepared, she sent the clients her PowerPoint slides ahead of time so they could see the data.

At the project update meeting, the Director of the management consulting firm, an authority figure who was highly respected by the clients, gave some opening remarks. His high status lent legitimacy to the progress update.

After the Director's remarks, Francesca took over for the remainder of the meeting. She was determined to persuade the client leads to continue the training program. Francesca felt like she had to fight for her intended outcome and this energized her. Both her physical and vocal presence conveyed energy and determination.

The total alignment of her intent, words, body, and voice led to full engagement and strengthened her presence. Francesca, a highly intelligent strategic communicator, had shifted into an impact mindset to get the results she wanted.

Knowing that her client expected a no-nonsense update, that's what she delivered.

Messaging to Persuade

Francesca conveyed two key points to the client leads: 1—why her team of consultants was not concerned about the low quantitative ratings, and 2—how the in-person training sessions were having a positive impact on the 200 global leaders who participated in them. She accomplished this through her verbal, vocal, and visual communication.

Verbally, she spoke their language by using quantitative metrics and referencing comments made by highly respected individuals who mattered most to the clients. Francesca deliberately spoke in short sentences because her clients valued concision.

Knowing that six of the seven key client leads had participated in the training, she directed specific questions to them so they could validate and reinforce her points. As examples, she asked one client lead, "Did you see something like that in your room?" and asked another, "What was that story you told me before?"

Vocally, she spoke in a louder volume than usual. From previous interactions with these clients, Francesca was aware that she needed to sound forceful and emphatic. She also deliberately varied her voice to emphasize key points.

Visually, she sat with an upright posture throughout the meeting. Francesca limited her smiling to reinforce the no-nonsense approach to the project status update. As she made each point, she looked directly at one of the client leads. Whenever she gave a specific example of the training's impact, she deliberately looked at one of the six client leads who had participated.

Attending to Each Decision-Maker

The one person in attendance who had not participated in the training session was Yuri. He was the head of this client group, the firm's Director of Strategy, and the right-hand man of the Chairman and CEO. Francesca kept a close watch on his responses, as well as those of the other six client leads.

To make sure she was addressing their questions and concerns, and getting their buy-in, Francesca paid close attention to their posture, body language, and facial expressions. By attending to the client leads, she saw that in the beginning of the meeting they were mostly leaning back in their seats. About mid-way through, they became more engaged in the conversation and sat more upright. Francesca also was aware that Yuri never looked at his phone but three of the other client leads checked their phones several times.

In addition to messaging congruously and being fully present, she focused on attending to create the kind of trusting partnership that was needed for getting approval to proceed with the project.

Intending to Get Client Approval

Francesca strategically used the IMPACT Paradigm practices.

Her clear intention—get client approval for moving forward with the training program and confirm a date for the next session—informed every word she spoke and every action she took.

By the end of the project update, Francesca got all of the client leads to agree to let the management consulting firm conduct a shortened training session. They agreed to change it from four hours to three hours. They agreed that the client leads would go through the three-hour training session with the team of consultants, then tell them what else needed to be cut if they felt it needed to be further shortened. After that, the consultants would move forward with the shortened training session for the rest of the firm's global leaders.

There was a big change from the beginning of the meeting when they were hesitant about continuing the project to the end of the meeting when they were nodding in response to Francesca's recap of each next step. Although they were packing up and not making eye contact, affirmative head nods from these client leads was a strong acknowledgement of their buy-in.

All left satisfied. The client's concerns were gone. The consultant's desired outcome was achieved. The training program lived on.

Situation 6: A Job Interview—Preparation for Music Auditions and Marketing Interviews

Auditions can be a terrifying experience. Most musicians who are trained put in weeks, months, sometimes even years of work to prepare for auditions in advance. Ruth, a trained musician, firmly believed that proper preparation was the only way she could walk into a music audition confident that she was ready.

After earning a degree in flute performance from a music conservatory, Ruth pursued a career path in the arts industry. She held arts administration positions in two non-profit organizations, managing activities, projects, and program development. Then, she went to business school and decided to recruit for a brand management position in a consumer products company.

To make the move from music to marketing, she applied the same disciplined approach to job interviews as she used for auditions.

Presence, Readiness, and Calm

In January 2016, Ruth was granted first-round interviews with five companies. Parallel to her experience in music, she did weeks of preparation.

Her preparation for each interview started with reading about the company, and getting a sense of its culture and core values. Aware that coming from such a different background required her professional story to have some relevance, she planned to use the company's core values to frame much of what she would say in her interviews. Ruth wanted to show each potential employer that she was ready to do what the company was doing.

Next, she analyzed the pros and cons of the five companies and one of them became her top choice. Not only was this company's location ideal and its training program for new hires excellent, all the people she met there during the recruiting process seemed passionate about what they did. Having known, used, and loved this particular company's products her whole life, Ruth felt she could easily market them.

She was scheduled for two days of interviews with three different people for a brand management position at this company.

Since Ruth had day classes, she devoted at least one hour, four nights a week to interview preparation. She diligently organized her preparation with a running Word document that had two to three stories she could tell for each question category, such as strengths, weaknesses, and leadership. If an interviewer asked her a question related to any of these topics, she could pull her answers from these stories. In addition, Ruth prepared answers to the five questions from the book *What Color is Your Parachute* that can apply to any interview. She also practiced a 60-second recap of her resume, also referred to as the "elevator pitch."

Aware that she would need to demonstrate to interviewers that she could think like a marketer, Ruth prepared for this too. She found it helpful to keep in mind the STAR framework—Situation, Task, Action, Result. She pulled out five different stories from her personal experience at work and at school, along with a task, actions, and a result for each. These stories took about two to three minutes to convey.

According to Ruth, "In the interview setting, people think they need to be in a zone but it's really just about being yourself." To that end, on the day of the interviews, Ruth put little emphasis on remembering what to say. Instead, she placed more importance on being calm so she could be herself when she interacted with the interviewers.

One hour before the first interview, she sat in a room and watched her favorite show on Netflix to feel relaxed. Ten minutes before the interview, she walked down to the assigned room and did breathing exercises. From her music training, Ruth knew that controlling her breathing steadies her nerves and makes her feel grounded. She also talked to other people in the room who looked nervous. It was beneficial to her, and probably to them, to think about things other than what was about to happen.

After the hours, days, and weeks of disciplined preparation, Ruth felt confident, able to be herself, and ready for whatever showed up during her interviews.

Messaging With Frameworks, Stories, and Examples

The first two interviews were with brand managers. They both asked questions about her personal brand and then technical marketing-specific questions.

Anticipating these two types of interview questions, Ruth was able to pull bits of information from what she had prepared in advance. These included the:

- company's core values
- stories using the STAR framework
- answers to the five questions from *What Color is Your Parachute*
- 3C concept of marketing strategy (customer, company, competitor)
- 4 Ps of marketing (product, place, price, promotion)
- 60-second recap of her resume (her "elevator pitch")
- relevant past experience

Her word choice was deliberate throughout these two interviews. She sat up tall and was cognizant of using her hands only when she wanted to reinforce her words. Ruth maintained eye contact when she spoke. During brief moments when she had to look away to think, she stopped speaking. As soon as she gathered her thoughts, she reconnected by looking the interviewer directly in the eyes and resumed speaking.

All went well during these two interviews. The very next day she was scheduled for her third and final interview. This one would be with a senior Human Resources executive.

Attending and Connecting with Purpose

Knowing how important it was for her to create a relaxed mindset, she again watched her favorite show on Netflix just before the interview.

When Ruth walked down the hall to the interview room, she noticed the Human Resource executive's business card, took it, and then went online to glance at her LinkedIn photo and profile. This helped her learn a bit about her final interviewer's background and work experience. Ruth made mental notes of this information so if asked at the end of the interview if she had any questions, she would have some.

From previous experiences, Ruth knew that interviews with Human Resource representatives tend to be very structured because they have a clear idea of what they are looking for in each candidate. That was the case with this interview.

The interviewer told Ruth right up front, "We're first going to talk about you and why you want to do this. Then we're going to talk about why marketing and what marketing means to you." She was looking for what the two brand managers may have missed.

They started with the personal brand piece and Ruth was very prepared for those questions. "Now we're going to talk about marketing," announced the interviewer.

Instead of asking one of the typical technical marketing interview questions, she said, "You don't have the word 'marketing' anywhere on your resume. Why should we even hire you?" The abruptness of this comment took Ruth aback, but she was prepared for it since she understood her own weakness. Until this moment, nobody had asked her this.

It was a flight or fight moment for Ruth. She really wanted this job and was determined to fight for it. Aware that this was a question that could stand between her and getting the offer, Ruth looked directly at her the whole time during this exchange.

"You are absolutely correct," answered Ruth. "The word 'marketing' is not on my resume, but if you look at every line and if you look at every role that I had, I was marketing a centuries-old art form to new audiences. So marketing is what I did. I lived it. I breathed it. If it weren't for the skills I was able to develop in my previous roles before going to business school, it wouldn't have been possible to do my work. This was all thanks to the fact that I had an understanding of the power of marketing this art form."

The interviewer nodded her head and said, "That is the best answer you could have possibly given me." Ruth smiled and thanked her.

Then the interviewer asked, "Do you have any questions for me?" Due to the positive response to her previous answer, Ruth took this question as an invitation to do something slightly different. She said, "I saw on your LinkedIn profile that you made the transition from finance to marketing. I'd love to know what that was like for you."

The interviewer paused, looked at Ruth, and said, "There's not been a single person who has asked me a question about me. Everybody has asked about the company. You're the first person who asked me a question about me." The interviewer smiled and then they had a conversation about her transition to marketing.

Attending to the interviewer by showing interest in her career not only set Ruth apart from other potential candidates, it also helped her build a connection with the interviewer.

During their conversation, she never lost sight of her intent. Ruth wanted the interviewer to walk away after their interaction knowing that she is the best person for the brand management position.

Ruth had the same feeling after the interview ended that she used to have after giving a solid performance at a music audition. It was an adrenalized feeling, a state of excitement, electricity, and empowerment.

The Human Resources executive called Ruth that evening to give her the job offer.

After a bit of conversation, she asked Ruth "Are you okay?" She responded, "I'm shaking, but I'm really happy." Then the Human Resources representative said, "Well, great. I'm going to give you some time to think about it." Ruth thanked her for this because she needed to regain her composure.

The next day, she accepted the position.

You read in Part One about attending and connecting—establishing and maintaining a positive relationship with the people involved in a communication interaction. In the two situations that follow, the first demonstrates how the IMPACT Paradigm principles of attending and connecting were the keys to networking success for Joseph, a military veteran; the second situation involves a television network executive, who used the principles of attending and connecting throughout a four-day negotiation with a film producer.

Situation 7: Networking—Spotting Commonalities, Building Common Ground

In Afghanistan, Joseph's Marine Corps platoon moved all over Helmand Province. They went from village to village, living out of their vehicles or out of abandoned compounds. As the rifle platoon commander, Joseph had to figure out how things worked in each location and how to interact with the locals. He was skilled at quickly getting a lay of the land.

Transitioning from the Marines to civilian life also would require Joseph to quickly get a lay of the land. However, this time, he needed to both adapt to a new environment and assimilate into this new culture.

He decided to go to networking events with military veterans to gather information about how he should act in a civilian, professional environment.

Attending Facilitates Learning

Veterans on Wall Street was a networking event for military veterans who worked in finance. Joseph, along with approximately 100 other people, attended this event.

He observed many interesting things there. Rank was not obvious. It was not easy to know who was a Managing Director and who was an Analyst. Nobody stood in the 'parade rest' position, with hands behind back, left foot 30 inches from the right foot, legs straight without locking the knees. People looked relaxed and at the same time, professional. Nobody said, "Yes, sir" or "No, sir." The attendees were talking to one another in a conversational manner. There seemed to be a natural, two-way flow.

After taking mental notes of how people were interacting, Joseph joined in. He asked a lot of questions and got people to talk to him about what they do. He listened intently to find out if what they were doing might be something he would be interested in as well.

Joseph went to a number of these military networking events at banks. Each time, he learned a lot by paying close attention to what people were doing and saying.

Some of the people he met at these events helped him put together a "less military, more civilian" resume. One person explained to him the importance of sending thank you notes to people he spoke with at networking events and to people who helped him. This was definitely not something people did in the military. "I would never send a thank you note to a General. It was out of my pay grade."

The learning and networking paid off. Joseph got an eight-week internship at a bank and applied to business school, where the process of recruiting for a full-time position began almost immediately.

Messaging to Create Connections

Joseph went to many school networking events with alumni recruiters from banks. He understood the importance of letting these bankers know that he had military and leadership experience, and most importantly, that he could adapt to a civilian professional culture. At these events, Joseph would sometimes see his fellow military veterans standing in "parade rest" position, giving "yes sir" or "no sir" answers in a networking circle. To Joseph, they seemed rigid and overly formal. He wondered if they would be able to adapt to a civilian environment.

At each networking event, the first thing Joseph did was scan the room. He looked for people who shared things in common with him. From his perspective, networking was all about making personal connections by attending to others and finding a commonality, then engaging with them in peer-to-peer conversations.

At one particular corporate presentation in business school, there were 20 alumni bankers. Some were Associates and others were Vice Presidents, Directors, and Managing Directors. Joseph quickly scanned the room and saw somebody with a "medium regulation" military haircut, which meant he was formerly a Marine. Joseph went right over to this recruiter, as did four other MBA students.

The first thing the recruiter said to the five students standing around him in the networking circle was, "Okay. What's everybody's background?" He pointed to Joseph, who said "I was in the Marine Corps." The recruiter said, "Oh, nice. What unit were you with?" That confirmed Joseph's guess that he too had been in the Marines. It turned out that Joseph and this recruiter had similar military backgrounds. They both went through training schools and Afghanistan at similar times.

After a few minutes of conversation in this networking circle, the recruiter gave each person his business card. Joseph told the recruiter "Nice meeting you. I would love to chat with you again." He responded, "Hit me up later." That was a good sign. Joseph would follow up with a thank you note and make sure he was aware that it was from a fellow Marine.

In another networking circle, Joseph recognized someone he had met a year earlier when he was a visiting business school applicant. This person, a member of the school's veterans club, had been Joseph's host and had taken him to audit one of the popular Investment Banking classes. Joseph couldn't quite place him, but went over to him anyway. He said, "Hi, I'm Joseph. Good to see you again." Joseph was hoping this person would remember and luckily, he did. "Yeah, nice to see you again." This was another result of successful scanning the room.

As soon as Joseph found a commonality with someone and verbally expressed it, he felt that he could take the ensuing conversation wherever it needed to go. The commonality created an immediate connection that put him and the other person at ease. They were "on the same playing field" as equals, co-creators of the conversation. When his networking conversations went from his background to the other person's background, and then to banking, that worked extremely well.

"Networking is about building relationships. A by-product might be that you get a job, or you get someone else a job, or even you end up getting that person a job," according to Joseph. He was comfortable that he would get a job if he did the networking properly.

Together, Developing Long-Term Connections

At a wine tasting event with a different bank, Joseph was in a circle with a group of students and two bankers. One was a Director, who graduated a decade ago; the other was an Associate, who graduated a year ago. Joseph listened attentively to the two of them speaking. He was impressed that the more senior person knew a lot about what the junior person was doing on the job, how she was doing, and why she had come to work at the company.

Joseph thought the Associate's accent could be a North Jersey or Long Island accent. Since he was from Long Island, he thought they might have that in common. When the networking circle was dwindling down, Joseph asked, "Where are you from?" She answered, "Westchester." He said, "Oh, Okay. I thought I heard an accent." Her response was, "I'm originally from Long Island." Following up on his hunch, he asked, "What part?"

It turned out that he and the Associate were from the same area. They proceeded to talk about common experiences. It was likely that after this event, the Associate from this bank would remember meeting the person who was from her town. Again, Joseph was able to find commonality with the other person and establish a connection that set him apart.

After several bankers from the same firm met Joseph and received his resume, they took his application to the hiring committee and vouched for him. That process resulted in Joseph getting to the final-round interview. First, he sat with the Vice

President who conducted the technical interview; and then, he met with a Managing Director, a woman who had been at the firm for 35 years.

At the technical interview, the Vice President gave nonverbal and verbal cues that led Joseph to believe he had been in the military. The Vice President asked Joseph if he had any questions at the end of the interview. "I got something wrong in the technical interview. Can you please explain what happened there?" Joseph wanted to show that he was interested in the right answer. After that, the Vice President asked, "Is there anything else?" Joseph asked, "Oh, did you serve?" "Yes, I was special forces . . ." Joseph shared that he, too, was in the Marines. They established a connection based on this commonality.

He then met with the Managing Director, who had a long history with the company. Joseph asked her about her experiences during the financial crash. "I have to ask. . . ." His question conveyed his sincere interest in her experience. Joseph was not afraid to ask questions that some people might think are taboo or too personal. As a result of his question, the Managing Director opened up and he learned a great deal about what was important to her. Their interaction became a relaxed conversation and Joseph knew they, too, were connecting.

Joseph was hired at the bank. But more than that, he became extremely skillful at building a large network and maintaining these connections.

"You never quite know when a relationship is going to help you out later on. It doesn't have to be a job. It could be a business opportunity, something for your kids, anything." He believes that "The more people you can call on or who can call on you, the better off it is." What matters most to Joseph is building his connections into long-term relationships.

Situation 8: A Negotiation—Trust is Essential

Could they reach an agreement about co-producing a documentary about three legendary, aging American filmmakers?

Eva, a television network executive from a global media and entertainment company, was responsible for negotiating the deal with Rafael, a noted feature film director/producer representing the filmmakers. Anticipating that Rafael might be skeptical about her company giving him creative freedom to tell the story the way he wanted it told, Eva knew she would have to gain his trust.

In preparation for their meeting, she collected background information about the three filmmakers so she could convey to Rafael her respect for their work and understanding of their role in the film industry. Eva also researched Rafael's background so she could talk about experiences with colleagues they had in common.

Additionally, she arranged to have one of her senior producers fly in from the West Coast to join her for the meeting in New York. John, a well-respected producer in the industry, would lend credibility to the project. He initially proposed the documentary project to Rafael, then brought in Eva as the Executive Producer, who persuaded the network to put up the money.

Eva invested significant time pre-negotiation to prepare for developing Rafael's trust.

The negotiation itself took four days.

Day 1: Attending

On day 1, Eva (5'1") and John (6'4") met with Rafael (6'7") at his foundation for filmmakers. Rafael, the president and co-founder of this foundation, was a towering figure with a booming voice. He gave them a tour of his building.

Eva, who was meeting Rafael for the first time, listened and periodically asked questions to show her interest and respect. As they walked from floor to floor, she smiled and nodded her head to encourage Rafael to elaborate on his stories about the foundation members, their film productions and the stars who appeared in them.

She saw him beaming with pride as he showed them photos of the filmmakers that lined the walls on every floor. She heard him over-enunciate each word. Eva thought he sounded as if he were giving a formal public speech in a large hall, rather than having a conversation with two people standing right next to him.

When they arrived in the conference room, Eva and John sat down. Rafael remained standing. He kept his distance from them in the room. He looked stiff and tense. Eva was aware of his lack of trust in her from the questions he asked. He assumed that she did not know certain details about the filmmakers that, in fact, she did.

Trust was a critical ingredient in this negotiation. The key to his willingness to openly share information about his interests and priorities about the production would be having a sufficient level of trust in Eva.

She cultivated a trusting relationship with him in three ways: first, by talking in great detail about the filmmakers, their creative approaches, and their activism in various causes; second, by listening to Rafael's concerns about the production; and third, by sharing information about her own background, their common experiences, and her knowledge and respect for the work of these legendary filmmakers.

Eventually, Rafael sat down. It was apparent to Eva that some trust was developing because Rafael looked more relaxed and sounded more conversational. The climate had changed. Rafael, Eva, and John were sharing stories and laughing together.

They were feeling a common bond, sharing their excitement about the documentary project.

Rafael's manner at the end of the meeting was markedly different than it had been two hours earlier. As he ushered Eva and John out of the building, they exchanged friendly parting words. All concurred that they looked forward to meeting the next day to start planning the production.

Day 2: Connecting

On day 2, they met in the same conference room at the foundation. Rafael's relaxed demeanor and conversational style at the end of day 1 continued throughout the meeting on day 2.

John, Eva, and Rafael sat comfortably at a round table, papers spread out, sharing ideas about the documentary. They discussed a schedule, plans for the crew, and a preliminary script. It was a relaxed, collaborative working session.

Based on their conversation about the production the previous day, Eva and John had come up with a preliminary script and showed it to Rafael. Then, they worked together and developed the script outline.

Eva also laid out a production plan and they discussed the parameters of the production. The more Eva and John listened to Rafael's recommendations, the more comfortable Rafael felt about the creative collaboration. Their strengthened connection helped them get the work done.

By the end of this meeting, they had agreed on their approach to the documentary production.

Days 3 and 4: Intending

On day 3, Eva came in ready to make the deal. Her intention was to leave this meeting with a signed contract. But Rafael came in ready to make demands. The critical issue was creative control.

Who would have the rights for final cut, the last version before the documentary goes on air? Rafael made his demand for the final cut and said he wouldn't sign the deal unless he had it. Eva was quite sure that her network had to have the final cut. They went back and forth about this.

Eva stayed calm, assuring Rafael that he could be involved in every edit session up to the final cut. Rafael reverted to the rigid stance and oratorical tone that he had on day 1, insisting on his demand for creative control. Periodically, John chimed in. He tried to reassure Rafael that Eva would make certain he was included in the creative process.

Tension was growing. Eva went into the room next door, called the Executive Vice President of Programming at the network, and told him Rafael wanted final cut. The Executive Vice President gave her a definitive decision. "Under no circumstances will the network give up the final cut." He also gave her a firm deadline to either close the deal or end the deal by the next day.

Soon after Eva returned to the conference room, Rafael announced in a loud voice that the meeting was over and that he was going to notify the three filmmakers.

Feeling pressure from Rafael and pressure from the network, Eva was concerned that the project might die. But Rafael continued the conversation with her on the phone that evening. He clearly wanted to bring the three legendary filmmakers together and make the documentary project happen. Throughout a series of phone calls, Eva maintained her dual focus on managing the relationship with Rafael and managing his satisfaction with the deal.

While she continued to reassure Rafael that he would be part of the entire process up to the final cut, she also signaled her willingness to make some salient concessions. Ultimately, she offered him final approval on script, music, crew, and schedule, but not on the final cut. In addition, she offered to give each of the filmmakers $20,000 for their appearance, as a token of trust.

On day 4, the final decision had to be made. Either Rafael would sign the deal or the network would withdraw its offer to produce the documentary.

His trust in her competence and character paid off in the end. They reached a mutually satisfactory agreement to co-produce a documentary about three American filmmakers to air on the television network, and signed the contract.

Eva had successfully attended to negotiating both the relationship and the final outcome.

You read in Part One about the final principle of the IMPACT Paradigm—together. The following section describes a popular professor's approach to giving keynote speeches at graduation ceremonies to thousands of people. Unlike popular belief that graduation addresses should focus only on the students, this professor aims to include everyone.

Situation 9: A Keynote Speech—Together, One with Thousands

Patrick, a very popular professor, is often invited to be the keynote speaker at college graduation ceremonies. He is disciplined about his process of coming together, being together, and staying together with the entire audience.

The graduation events take place in large venues, such as Radio City Music Hall, with a seating capacity of over 6,000. The audiences tend to be very diverse. The format typically includes numerous speeches by administrators and students, a keynote speech delivered by a non-academic person, and a keynote speech delivered by an academic, Patrick.

Unlike many people who speak at graduation events, Patrick speaks to the graduates and to everyone else who is in the audience. He cares about the audience, which is why he wants them to pay attention throughout his speech and remember what he says.

Messaging, "Fresh Like Sushi"

His approach to planning keynote speeches is unique.

The first step involves seeing who all the other speakers are, especially the outside non-academic speaker. He researches the outside speaker's recent graduation speeches on YouTube videos. This gives him a hint of what that person's content will be. Patrick has found over the years that most speakers tend to continue essentially the same speech, as long as it's relevant.

One of his key objectives when putting together a speech is to know enough about what others might say so he can avoid being repetitious and can engage the audience throughout his speech.

The second step involves making a list of what he wants to talk about. Ideally, he wants to end up with four main thoughts. This makes it easier for him to remember because he never uses notes for his keynote speeches. It also makes it easier for the audience to remember. Patrick believes that less is more when it comes to effective, memorable messaging.

How does he prepare the four thoughts? Months in advance of the speech, he starts thinking about as many as sixteen different ideas. Over time, he tries delivering them in different ways, reflecting on what it is that he most wants to say. By practicing, he gets comfortable with them. Eventually, he trims them down to six. He practices these six ideas over and over in his head or out loud, sitting on a train, driving in a car, or whenever he possibly can.

The third step of his planning process, when the final four emerge, takes place on the way to the event. Patrick listens to what he calls "*current* current events." He wants his verbal messaging to be relevant. "I like to keep it fresh like sushi," he says. Patrick listens to the news of the day and thinks about which of the six selected topics are most relevant to the audience. Which will they be most interested in? Which will they identify with immediately because it's happening today?

The fourth step takes place when he arrives at the graduation venue. He continues practicing and rehearsing the speech in his mind. No notes. Patrick knows he can't possibly make a mistake because nobody would know anyway since they have no idea what he is going to talk about beforehand. For that reason, instead of worrying, he spends his time practicing his message.

Patrick organizes his keynote speeches with a beginning, middle, and end—a structure that is both logically and psychologically satisfying.

As an example, he started one graduation speech with a story, "I was reading a book as I came in on the train and I came across the Seven Deadly Sins." That grabbed everyone's attention. Knowing the importance of previewing what will follow in the speech at the beginning, he went on to say, "That's too many for this speech so let's eliminate three and talk about the four that will matter to you for the rest of your life." Then he made it clear why they should listen, "It's really important because it seems like we have no ethics in the world anymore, so you are going to have to figure out how to get that back for all of us." He proceeded to review the four deadly sins, one by one, with amusing anecdotes to make them more memorable.

In the middle of a different graduation speech, he talked about change and disruption. "We live in a disruptive world. You're going to be living in a more disruptive world." He followed that up with examples, "The pope is disruptive . . . technology is disruptive . . . this person is disruptive . . ." Patrick had something for everyone in the audience so they would understand what he was talking about. He ended by talking about the importance of change and congratulating the entire audience. With memorable words and large gestures that acknowledged everyone, "From the best, to the best, all the best."

In large venues, his speeches are delivered standing in a stable position behind a podium. Staying close to the microphone so everyone can hear every word limits his movements, but he uses facial expressions and upper body gestures that can be seen projected on screens throughout the venue. When Patrick looks out, it's too dark to see faces. In this context where he can't see the audience, he does not look for immediate feedback. Instead, he remains totally focused on what he wants to convey to the audience.

His manner of speaking is conversational, expressive, emphatic, and energetic. Patrick uses the same vocal delivery when he is speaking one-on-one, and to small and large group audiences. He believes, "It's easier that way."

Be Present, Connect Now, Remember Always

To ensure his own full engagement and the full engagement of the entire audience during the speech, Patrick has a set of guidelines that he follows on the day of the keynote.

1. Arrive at the space and go on stage ahead of time. Stand there for five minutes, at least. Do a sound test and ask for the lights to be turned on to get comfortable with the ambiance in the room.

2. Watch the audience when marching down the long aisle to get to the seat on stage. Pay attention to who is in the audience and the diversity in the room.

3. Listen closely to the other speeches. Eliminate some topics and hone down to the final four topics. Add or delete in the moment.

4. Begin the keynote speech by going to the podium and saying nothing for a few moments. In silence, look around the entire room to get the audience ready.

5. Open with a positive, friendly comment—something relevant that makes the students laugh and gets the family members wondering what caused the laughter.

6. Start weaving in the four topics and take deliberate pauses when looking for the next thing to say.

7. Make sure to speak to everyone in the room so that everyone listens.

8. Keep the audience entertained with stories and references to "*current* current events" that keep it fresh.

9. Maintain focus on the four topics so the audience remembers the key takeaways—the "life lessons."

10. Cap the speech at the end with a memorable and kind way to congratulate the entire audience.

Years after graduation, alumni talk about the stories told and the life lessons offered by Patrick in his graduation speeches. They remember.

The discipline of preparing and delivering a keynote speech, according to Patrick, is to: "Always think about the entire audience and include everyone." As a result, the speaker and the audience connect and share a memorable experience, together.

Conclusion

Throughout this chapter, we have focused on how the IMPACT Paradigm applies to a range of different types of communication interactions. By now, we know that the principles of intending, messaging, presence, attending, connecting, and together apply whether working in a bank, a consumer goods company, a hospital, an educational institution, or any other organizational context. We also know that all of these principles are essential for making purposeful communication effective.

Here is a checklist of questions to keep in mind when reflecting on communication interactions at work.

Intending

- Do I have a clear intention for this interaction?
- Am I allowing unexpected reactions to interfere with my focus on intending throughout the interaction?

Messaging

- Is my visual, vocal, and verbal communication congruous?
- Is my verbal messaging clear and concise or confusing, rambling, and disjointed?

Presence

- How am I showing up in this interaction?
- Do I feel something getting in the way of my being fully present, physically and vocally?

Attending

- Am I paying attention to the other person with whom I'm interacting?
- Is my internal focus preventing me from attending to the other person's words, body language, and paralanguage?

Connecting

- Have I established a connection with the other(s) in this interaction?
- Am I doing anything to hinder connecting throughout the interaction?

Together

- Is this a conversational interaction?
- Am I "talking at others" instead of engaging in a conversation together?

4

COMMON CONCERNS OF COMMUNICATORS

We can all become more effective strategic communicators by using the IMPACT Paradigm. As I've seen in my work with graduate students and working professionals, and the previous chapter illustrated, the six impact principles can be used to great effect in any kind of communication interaction, in any work setting, with any size audience. The more we apply these principles, the more comfortable and confident we become in their use. This takes commitment, sustained effort, and an impact mindset.

Why is it important to adopt an impact mindset, a way of thinking about our communication practices? It enables us to recognize how we approach communication interactions to achieve desired results, as well as reframe how we think about common communication concerns and beliefs that may get in our way of becoming the most strategic communicators we can be.

Among the common concerns and limiting beliefs we can reframe with an impact mindset are:

- Feeling Nervous: Reframe Anxiety to Energy
- Becoming Distracted: Reframe Reactivity to Proactivity

- Experiencing Overwhelm: Reframe Misstep to Mastery

- Lacking Confidence: Reframe Self-Doubt to Self-Assurance

- Paying Attention to Imperfections: Reframe Internal to External Focus

- Being Inarticulate: Reframe Faltering Speech to Flowing Conversation

- Holding Back: Reframe Inaction to Action

In this chapter, we first consider each of these concerns and beliefs that make strategic communication harder than it need be. Second, we reframe each one, giving a more helpful way of understanding it. Third, we reorient the approach to a particular aspect of communicating purposefully, specifying actions to maximize impact. Fourth, we revisit the examples in Chapter 3 that illustrate how individuals used the IMPACT Paradigm to get results at work. Fifth and last, we realize how reframing each concern, reorienting our approach, and adopting the impact mindset increase our communication effectiveness.

From Anxious to Energized
The Impact Mindset for Achieving Readiness

"*I get nervous*" often is a response to a range of physical sensations that occur moments before speaking, such as heart pounding, blood rushing to the face, legs and hands tingling. These physical responses are natural and can be brought under control and understood in a way that is productive, rather than debilitating: "I feel physically and mentally ready to speak."

Reframe: "I feel physically and mentally ready."

Reorient: Channel this energy into a purposeful conversation—get centered, grounded, and deliberately choose first words.

Speaking is both a physical and a mental activity. How we channel our physical energy, along with how we represent the act of speaking in our own minds, influences how we engage in communication interactions.

We can manage speaking anxiety by first acknowledging that a surge of energy is natural, then recognizing it as readiness and excitement that we can channel into a purposeful conversation. Every one of us can choose to put this vital energy to use by directing it toward getting ready, staying alert, and achieving our desired outcome.

Readiness requires getting centered and grounded. The IMPACT Paradigm practices teach us how to find a neutral, relaxed posture, and breathe properly, slowly and deeply. These physical actions give us a sense of control and stability that facilitates a relaxed and focused state of mind. Since the anticipation period before speaking, as well as the first few moments of speaking, tend to be the most challenging, planning the first words we want to say (whenever possible) is also an effective way to gain control and composure. Once we begin, it gets easier from then on.

To maximize impact and achieve intended outcomes, it is essential to use our body and mind. We need to get ready and then start strong with a positive mental state. Then, we can remain strong throughout the communication interaction. Not only does this convey our confidence and competence, it also strengthens our presence.

Revisit: Ruth's Job Interviews—Preparation for Music Auditions and Marketing Interviews (Chapter 3).

On the day of the interviews, Ruth put little emphasis on remembering what to say. Instead, she placed more importance on being calm so she could be herself when she interacted with the interviewers.

One hour before the first interview, she sat in a room and watched her favorite show on Netflix to feel relaxed. Ten minutes before the interview, she walked down to the assigned room and did breathing exercises. From her music training, Ruth knew that controlling her breathing steadies her nerves and makes her feel grounded.

Realize: It's natural and necessary to feel energized before speaking.

When we experience physical responses to a speaking opportunity, view this as a positive sign of readiness for the communication interaction.

From Reactive to Proactive
The Impact Mindset for Intending Throughout

"*I get distracted*" tends to happen when so much attention is placed on others' reaction that the speaker and, as a consequence, the message get derailed. Instead, "I remain proactive, focused on my intent" guides words and actions, without losing sight of the desired outcome.

Reframe: "I remain proactive, focused on my intent."

Reorient: Have a clear intent to inform the choice of words and actions.

Intending throughout a communication interaction serves us in many ways. It enables us to stay in control. It keeps us on course. It allows us to make minor adjustments along the way without losing focus on what we want others to know, or do, or feel as a result of our communication.

When listeners fidget or avoid making eye contact, we can avoid becoming distracted by remaining focused on intending. It is important to "read the room," but only as it relates to making the adjustments needed to take listeners from Point A (where they are when the interaction starts) to Point B (where we want to take them at the end of the interaction).

Identifying a clear intention is crucial because it informs every aspect of our communication. The IMPACT Paradigm practices teach us how to express our intention, verbally, visually, and vocally. Our messaging changes when our intention changes. We convey our intent through words, vocal delivery, facial expressions, and body language.

Engaging in intending throughout the communication not only keeps us on point, it supports us in achieving our desired outcomes.

Revisit: Francesca's Project Update—High Stakes for a Consultant (Chapter 3).
Francesca strategically used the IMPACT Paradigm practices.

Her clear intention—get client approval for moving forward with the training program and confirm a date for the next session—informed every word she spoke and every action she took.

By the end of the project update, Francesca got all of the client leads to agree to let the management consulting firm conduct a shortened training session. They agreed to change it from four hours to three hours. They agreed that the client leads would go through the three-hour training session with the team of consultants, then tell them what else needed to be cut if they felt it needed to be further shortened. After that, the consultants would move forward with the shortened training session for the rest of the firm's global leaders.

Realize: For strategic communicators, intending is essential from beginning to end of the interaction.

Remain focused on expressing a clear intent throughout the communication, keeping in mind that listeners will inevitably display a range of behaviors.

From Misstep to Mastery
The Impact Mindset for Messaging Purposefully

"*I get overwhelmed*" is an experience of trying to get all the thoughts running through the mind out at once to avoid making the dreaded mistake of forgetting to say one or more things. To manage the delivery of the message and maximize its impact, strategic communicators "complete one thought at a time, and use silence effectively."

Reframe: "Complete one thought at a time."

Reorient: Take pauses to manage the delivery of the message.

Messaging that has impact is extremely important and necessary for strategic communication at work. To get the results we want requires delivering clear, concise, and comprehensible verbal messages.

We can get all our thoughts out without getting overwhelmed by focusing on one thought at a time and pausing. This makes it easy for others to understand. Communicating one complete thought and then pausing also enables us to feel in control and effectively manage our delivery.

Resisting the urge to speak continuously, as well as eliminating filler words ("um," "er," "ah") that replace pauses, becomes easier as we become more comfortable with silence. The IMPACT Paradigm practices teach us when to allow silence. Pausing before speaking benefits both speakers and listeners. Taking a pause after one complete thought gives speakers time to gather their thoughts before moving on to the next thought. It also provides listeners with a brief moment to reflect on what was just said and await what will be said next.

Pausing effectively after delivering a complete thought not only signals a speaker's confidence, it also keeps listeners engaged.

Revisit: Patrick's Keynote Speech—Together, One with Thousands (Chapter 3)

To ensure his own full engagement and the full engagement of the entire audience during the speech, Patrick has a set of guidelines that he follows on the day of the keynote.

- *Begin the keynote speech by going to the podium and saying nothing for a few moments. In silence, look around the entire room to get the audience ready.*

- *Open with a positive, friendly comment—something relevant that makes the students laugh and gets the family members wondering what caused the laughter.*

- *Start weaving in the four topics and take deliberate pauses when looking for the next thing to say.*

Realize: Focusing on the clear and complete expression of each individual thought is most important.

Leverage the power of pauses to stay in control of messaging and increase the engagement of listeners.

From Self-Doubting to Self-Assured
The Impact Mindset for Being Present

"*I'm not confident*" is a common concern. Most often, it takes a minor adjustment of physical behavior and mindset to show up with more confidence. Then, it becomes possible to have the experience that "I am fully present" in the moment.

Reframe: "I am fully present."

Reorient: Make minor adjustments to enhance presence.

When we are fully present in an interaction, people see it, hear it, and respond to it. We convey our confidence, conviction, and competence through our communication behavior. When we are not fully present, people know it; but the good news is that we can change that by making small adjustments to our physical and vocal behavior.

We can indicate our overall attitude, and level of comfort, confidence, and professionalism by our posture. It is often the first thing people notice about us. How we take up the space around us significantly affects how confident we look. We also can send signals to ourselves and others through our facial expressions and voice tone. If we look and sound bored, people react in kind. If we choose behaviors that project confidence and exhibit presence, people are drawn in.

Enhancing our presence is a capability that we all have. The impact mindset and IMPACT Paradigm practices teach us how to become more fully aware of what is going on moment to moment and how to strengthen our presence through aligning, breathing, grounding, occupying space, and incorporating vocal variety.

Making small changes can make a big difference in how we show up to ourselves and to others.

Revisit: Joni's Corporate Pitch—Requesting $1,000,000 (Chapter 3).
Sitting up straight on the edge of her chair, close to the table, Joni remained alert. Her presence was strong throughout the pitch.

Joni knew the proposal so well that she was able to stay focused on her desired outcome, while paying attention to the behavior of people in the room. She was able to communicate the passion and excitement of the team to do the work on behalf of the business unit, while engaging the President and CFO throughout the pitch.

Being present—mind and body—throughout the pitch clearly had an impact . . . The President and CFO agreed that this reputation campaign should be supported with an investment of one million dollars.

Realize: Using the impact mindset and IMPACT Paradigm principles, we can project confidence and increase our physical and vocal presence.

At any given moment, we can self-correct by making minor adjustments that influence how we show up and express ourselves.

From Internal to External Focus
The Impact Mindset for Attending and Connecting

"*I judge myself*" arises from being hyperaware of one's own imperfections and being highly self-critical. A way to avoid falling into this negative self-judgment trap during communication interactions is to shift from an internal focus on one's own experience to an external focus on others' experience. Since the results of communication are situated in the responses received by others, the salient point for strategic communicators to remember is that: "It's not about me, it's about what the other person receives."

Reframe: "It's not about me, it's about what the other person receives."

Reorient: Attend to the other person by focusing out and watching each message land.

The importance of focusing out cannot be overstated. It accomplishes many things that support effective communication.

It gives us a welcome relief from overly harsh self-criticism that can cause us to dread or completely avoid certain types of communication interactions. It also shows that we are paying attention to others while they take in what we have to say, and that we care about their responses. As a result of focusing on the other person, we establish a connection with them that can be maintained throughout the communication interaction.

We can move our attention off of the speaker and on to the listener by watching how each one of our messages is received. This process of looking at one person for one complete thought has a powerful effect. By showing our interest in the listener, we establish a connection, and facilitate a back and forth flow of communication. The listener knows we expect engagement.

Engaging others fully in every communication requires an external focus. The IMPACT Paradigm practices teach us how to focus our attention outward, observing and listening to others, and how to remain in a state of relaxed awareness while establishing and maintaining connection.

Revisit: Jenna's Workplace Conversation—Managing Up (Chapter 3).
Jenna deliberately maintained an outward focus throughout their conversation so she could see his movements and facial expressions, and know when it was appropriate to ask questions or respond with comments. By visually attending and actively listening to him, she was able to direct the conversation toward the overall situation at the bank. She asked him where he thought the team was going in light of all the changes, and how the team could function in the future.

They shared how they approach their work, how they see them-selves, and how they handle their workflow. They also talked about expectations and the challenges of team management.

The connection Jenna established by attending to Dave remained strong throughout. Their conversation flowed naturally and easily from her experience since the fallout of the financial crisis to his experience, and then to their shared experience.

Realize: Focusing on others takes attention off of ourselves.

Switch to an external focus to establish and maintain connection with others.

From Faltering to Flowing
The Impact Mindset for Conversing Together

"*I can't find the right words.*" Instead of worrying about coming up with the perfect word or turn of phrase, express ideas naturally as in a conversation: "Make it a conversation."

Reframe: "Make it a conversation."

Reorient: Approach each communication as a conversational interaction.

Conversation, a form of spoken communication between two or more people, is familiar to all of us. Throughout the course of a typical work day, we have many conversations with individuals and groups of people to exchange information, thoughts, feelings, and ideas. When we engage in conversation, we are not scripted.

We can stop worrying about coming across as inarticulate by first appreciating that there is no one right way to express an idea, then approaching each communication as a conversational interaction. In these interpersonal exchanges, everyday words are spoken in a tone that is relaxed and casual. We all have lots of experience with this kind of conversational interaction.

As noted earlier, the word *conversation* means "to move together." The IMPACT Paradigm practices teach us how to have engaging interactions that achieve desired outcomes within a reciprocal relationship. These intentional interchanges, whether one-on-one or one-to-many, are collaborative and dynamic. One message builds on the next with the aim of reaching a mutual understanding and a specific end point. To accomplish this, we follow a simple beginning-middle-end structure, a critical element of effective conversational interactions. Organizing our messaging not only informs the flow of ideas, it also facilitates creating shared meaning, achieving outcomes, and taking informed action, together.

Approaching our communication as we would a conversation enables us to interact in a way that is comfortable and familiar to us. In purposeful conversations, what matters most is staying connected to the other person and having a progression of exchanges in support of intended outcomes.

Revisit: Joseph's Networking—Spotting Commonalities, Building Common Ground (Chapter 3).
As soon as Joseph found a commonality with someone and verbally expressed it, he felt that he could take the ensuing conversation wherever it needed to go. The commonality created an immediate connection that put him and the other person at ease. They were "on the same playing field" as equals, co-creators of the conversation. When his networking conversations went from his background to the other person's background, and then to banking, that worked extremely well.

Realize: We already know how to have a conversation, together.

Think of communication as conversation that allows us to interact with others in a way that engages them and puts us at ease.

From Inaction to Action
The Impact Mindset for Achieving Outcomes

"*I don't think I can do it differently.*" Whenever that thought comes to mind, reset, and remember to "Engage in the IMPACT practices" to increase communication effectiveness.

Reframe: "Engage in the IMPACT practices."

Reorient: Check in, re-engage, and commit to each practice.

Revisit: (Chapter 3)

Intending—Jenna's Workplace Conversation
The only thing Jenna did to prepare for this conversation was focus on her intent—to get approval from Dave to relinquish her responsibility for making the revisions on every compliance report generated by the team. She knew it would be critical to stick to her intent throughout the conversation to keep it on course and achieve her desired outcome.

Messaging—Alex's Presentation
Alex delivered a memorable presentation and was effective in achieving his intended outcome: to call attention to the existence and contribution of the title company and increase appreciation for the work of its employees. Without using notes or slides, he successfully accomplished this by first grabbing the audience's attention with a surprising, entertaining, light-hearted opening. Once he had their attention, he kept their interest with his congruous messaging and high-energy delivery throughout the presentation.

Presence—Francesca's Project Update
The total alignment of her intent, words, body, and voice led to full engagement and strengthened her presence. Francesca, a highly intelligent

strategic communicator, had shifted into an impact mindset to get the results she wanted. Knowing that her client expected a no-nonsense update, that's what she delivered.

Attending—Eva's Negotiation

She saw him beaming with pride as he showed them photos of the filmmakers that lined the walls on every floor. She heard him over-enunciate each word. Eva thought he sounded as if he were giving a formal public speech in a large hall, rather than having a conversation with two people standing right next to him. When they arrived in the conference room, Eva and John sat down . . . Eventually, Rafael sat down. It was apparent to Eva that some trust was developing because Rafael looked more relaxed and sounded more conversational.

Connecting—Joseph's Networking

Joseph was hired at the bank. But more than that, he became extremely skillful at building a large network and maintaining these connections. "You never quite know when a relationship is going to help you out later on. It doesn't have to be a job. It could be a business opportunity, something for your kids, anything." He believes that "The more people you can call on or who can call on you, the better off it is." What matters most to Joseph is building his connections into long-term relationships.

Together—Dr. Mackay's Small Group Meeting

The upshot of the meeting was an agreement to let the physician take the new, more favorable option and work out specific action steps with the Chairman of Anesthesia. They decided together that Dr. Farr would continue in his position and meet monthly with the Chairman of Anesthesia. Each month, the Chairman would report on Dr. Farr's performance using the Focused Professional Practice Evaluation process. For six months, every single one of Dr. Farr's anesthesia records would be audited . . . The outcome was far better than anyone expected. The performance and behavior problems stopped entirely. The physician kept his word and kept his job.

Realize: The IMPACT Paradigm provides practical guidance for increasing communication effectiveness.

Commit to applying the impact principles in everyday communication interactions.

Conclusion

Here is the bottom line: we can be more confident, more engaging, and more effective when we apply the IMPACT Paradigm principles and adopt the impact mindset.

The impact mindset is based on the belief that we can direct our thoughts and actions to achieve results and maximize impact when we communicate. It comes into play in all types of communication interactions, from workplace conversations and meetings, to presentations and speeches.

As we've seen, the impact mindset reframes how we think about common communication concerns and limiting beliefs:

- Feeling Nervous: Reframe Anxiety to Energy

  The Impact Mindset for Achieving Readiness

- Becoming Distracted: Reframe Reactivity to Proactivity

  The Impact Mindset for Intending Throughout

- Experiencing Overwhelm: Reframe Misstep to Mastery

  The Impact Mindset for Messaging Purposefully

- Lacking Confidence: Reframe Self-Doubt to Self-Assurance

  The Impact Mindset for Being Present

- Paying Attention to Imperfections: Reframe Internal to External Focus

  The Impact Mindset for Attending to and Connecting with Others

- Being Inarticulate: Reframe Faltering Speech to Flowing Conversation

  The Impact Mindset for Conversing Together

- Holding Back: Reframe Inaction to Action

  The Impact Mindset for Achieving Outcomes

When we adopt an impact mindset, with its focus on outcomes, we recognize the importance of a clear intention, congruent verbal and non-verbal communication, attentiveness to and connection with others. In the impact mindset, we understand the power of presence and the power of conversation.

It is one thing to believe that effective communication is about outcomes and impact. It is another thing to integrate the skills that are needed to achieve intended outcomes and maximize the impact of our communication. That takes practice.

In the final two chapters of this book, I provide detailed instructions for practice exercises. Each exercise relates to one or more of the IMPACT Paradigm principles—intending, messaging, presence, attending, connecting, together.

With focused practice, we become more comfortable in doing each activity. The more we practice, the more easily we can integrate these skills in our everyday interactions. By continuing our practice, we develop new habits that increase our communication effectiveness. Eventually, applying the IMPACT Paradigm to our communication interactions at work becomes second nature.

PART THREE
Practicing

5

IMPACT EXERCISES

Why Engage in Focused Practice of IMPACT Exercises?

The twenty curated exercises in this chapter are designed for focused practice of essential elements of the IMPACT Paradigm. Each exercise isolates certain skills that when mastered increase our communication competence. Through focused practice, we build competence. We can progress through the four stages of learning: from unconscious incompetence (unaware of the skill and lack of proficiency) to conscious incompetence (aware of the skill but not yet proficient), then to conscious competence (able to use the skill but only with effort), and eventually to unconscious competence (the skill becomes automatic—"second nature").

In essence, these IMPACT Exercises provide us with a communication workout. Repetition of these twenty selected exercises builds our muscle memory and creates new habits. It ensures that the skills we practice will be lasting. By prioritizing focused practice of these exercises, we are committing to strengthening our ability to achieve maximum impact when we communicate at work.

How do we Engage in Focused Practice of IMPACT Exercises?

In this chapter, there are detailed instructions for each exercise. There are also questions for each exercise so we can do periodic check-ins and make self-corrections anytime throughout the day. That way, we are building our skill set, incorporating these skills in in our everyday interactions at work, and continuously improving.

We become our own coaches during focused practice of the IMPACT Exercises. A recommended strategy is to start by doing them in sequence to become familiar with each exercise; then, select one or two exercises at a time to practice and eventually master the set of skills involved.

When we engage in communication interactions at work and become aware that we are not using a particular skill that we practiced, then self-correct on the spot. Simply notice, make the required adjustment, and continue engaging in the interaction.

What are the 20 IMPACT Exercises?

Our focus for each exercise is on skills related to one or more of the six IMPACT Paradigm principles. This focus is shown by the white letters on the graphic identifier above the instructions.

The first set of exercises in this series focuses on IMP (Intending, Messaging, and Presence). We do each of these exercises on our own.

- Exercises 1 through 6 focus on MP (Messaging and Presence).

- Exercises 7 through 9 focus on IMP (Intending, Messaging, and Presence).

The second set of exercises in this series focuses on IMPA (Intending, Messaging, Presence, and Attending). These exercises involve interacting with other people.

- Exercises 10 through 12 focus on MA (Messaging and Attending).
- Exercises 13 through 15 focus on IMPA (Intending, Messaging, Presence, and Attending).

The third and final set of exercises in this series focuses on IMPACT—all six IMPACT Paradigm practices. Exercises 16 through 20 involve communication interactions with one or more people.

Note: If you have had any recent physical problems, adapt these exercises to your physical ability.

TABLE 5.1 IMPACT Exercises						
IMPACT Exercise	*Intending*	*Messaging*	*Presence*	*Attending*	*Connecting*	*Together*
1. Finding Center		✗	✗			
2. Releasing Tension		✗	✗			
3. Breathing Deeply		✗	✗			
4. Speaking Clearly		✗	✗			
5. Varying the Voice		✗	✗			
6. Freeing the Voice		✗	✗			
7. Speaking with the Body	✗	✗	✗			
8. Visualizing	✗	✗	✗			
9. Preparing	✗	✗	✗			
10. Observing		✗		✗		
11. Describing Details		✗		✗		
12. Listening		✗		✗		
13. Calming the Mind			✗			
14. Planning First Words	✗	✗		✗		
15. Moving from Scripted to Unscripted	✗	✗				
16. Shortening Sentences	✗	✗	✗	✗	✗	✗
17. Establishing Connection	✗	✗	✗	✗	✗	✗
18. Speaking with Purpose	✗	✗	✗	✗	✗	✗
19. Structuring Effectively	✗	✗	✗	✗	✗	✗
20. Speaking Conversationally	✗	✗	✗	✗	✗	✗

Focus for Exercise #1: Finding Center

Get grounded and stable, maintain proper alignment, and feel centered. The center is a position of complete physical balance, the ideal position of readiness for your body and voice. In this vital center position, you can gather your energy together before moving into action.

Position of Balance, Strength, and Readiness

- Starting with feet parallel, hip-width apart, lift toes, spread and place feet on the floor keeping toes apart. Shift weight slightly forward onto balls of feet so you feel the big toes.

- Knees slightly bent, unlocked.

- Rock pelvis forward and back to find centered position, not forward but resting comfortably with the weight of the hips directly over the feet.

- Spine up, shoulders released, throat relaxed.

- Head balanced on top of the spine, jaw relaxed, eyes looking forward.

- Keep breathing.

Periodically Check In

- ✓ Is my weight evenly distributed throughout my body?
- ✓ Are my feet off balance?
- ✓ Are my hips off center?
- ✓ Is my pelvis pushed forward or pulled back?

✓ Is my spine rigid or slumped?

✓ Are my shoulders hunched forward or pulled back?

✓ Are my knees locked?

✓ Is my head down or pulled forward or back?

✓ Am I looking at the floor?

Self-Correct

Return to your centered position.

Focus for Exercise #2: Releasing Tension

Loosen up and prepare to use facial expressions, natural gestures, and purposeful movement when communicating. The tensions that reside throughout your body can interfere with breathing and speaking. Releasing useless tensions allows your whole body to engage naturally in the act of speaking.

Head and Neck

- Standing with feet hip-width apart, let head drop down until chin touches chest.
- Rotate left ear to left shoulder, then right ear to right shoulder.
- Lift head until it feels balanced on top of spine.
- Let head gently fall back, keeping your jaw free.
- Lift head until it feels balanced on top of spine.

Eyes and Face

- Alternate between squinting and wide eyes.
- Alternate between your biggest facial expression (surprise) and your smallest (sour).

Tongue, Lips, and Jaw

- Stretch tongue to your nose, chin, and cheeks.
- Blow air through lips to make a motorboat sound.
- Mimic chewing a very large piece of gum.

Shoulders and Arms

- Stand with arms down. Lift and drop the shoulders.

- Circle shoulders clockwise, then counter-clockwise.

- Circle right arm clockwise, as if throwing a ball underhand. Repeat with left arm.

- Hold hands behind your back. Gently lift arms away from your back and then release.

Wrists and Fingers

- Rotate wrists in circular motion. Reverse direction.

- Vigorously shake both hands as if you are shaking off water from your fingers.

Back and Chest

- Mimic hugging a tree to stretch out the back muscles.

- Mimic crushing an orange between your shoulder blades to stretch out the chest.

Legs, Knees, and Feet

- Stand in place and shake out any tension in legs. Then gently bounce your knees. Return to standing position without locking the knees.

- Lift one foot, rotate ankle. Repeat with other foot.

- Lift one foot, point toes down, and then flex with heel reaching down and toes pointing up. Repeat with other foot.

Periodically Check In

- ✓ Are my neck and shoulders tense or relaxed?
- ✓ Am I tensing up the muscles in my face?
- ✓ Am I holding tension in any other part of my body?
- ✓ Is my facial expression fixed or am I varying my facial expression?
- ✓ Am I seeing the person with whom I'm speaking or am I looking away?
- ✓ Is my mouth moving sufficiently to clearly articulate every word?
- ✓ Are my hands moving in a natural, conversational way?
- ✓ Am I breathing deeply?
- ✓ Am I maintaining good posture?

Self-Correct

Bring attention to a part of your body that feels tense, exaggerate the tension for a moment, and then let the tension go.

Focus for Exercise #3: Breathing Deeply

Control diaphragmatic breathing to feel calm and support your voice. Lack of breath and support, the muscular means of controlling breath, is the biggest problem most speakers have. To harness the power of your breath and project vocal presence, you need to have a strong, flexible breath and support system.

Slow Breath

- Inhale slowly through the nose.
- Exhale slowly through the nose.

Calming Breath—4–7–8

- Exhale completely through your mouth, making an audible "whoosh" sound.
- Inhale quietly through your nose, mouth closed, for a count of 4.
- Hold your breath for a count of 7. (Gradually build up to this count, if necessary.)
- Exhale completely through your mouth, making a "whoosh" sound, for a count of 8.
- Inhale again for a count of 4, hold for a count of 7, exhale for a count of 8.
- Repeat the above cycle (4–7–8) two more times for a total of four complete breaths.

Core Breath

- Sitting in a chair, relax your shoulders.

- Place one hand on your chest and the other hand on your abdomen.

- Inhale gently through your nose for a count of two. The hand on your abdomen should rise and the hand on your chest should move very little.

- Exhale through your mouth, pushing out as much air as you can while contracting the abdominal muscles. The hand on your abdomen should move in as you exhale and the hand on your chest should move very little.

- Continue breathing in through the nose and out through the mouth.

- Try this lying down, hand on your abdomen. Hand rises as you inhale, lowers as you exhale.

Core Breath—5–5–5

- Standing up, begin by relaxing your body and making sure your posture is aligned.

- Place your hand on your abdomen.

- Inhale gently through your nose for a count of 5. Notice how your hand rises as your diaphragm (the muscle separating the chest and abdominal cavities) expands.

- Hold the breath for a count of 5.

- Exhale through your mouth for a count of 5 while gently pressing on the abdomen.

- Repeat entire process from the beginning, adding an audible sigh when you exhale.

Breath Control

- Sitting, rest arms on knees or arms of chair, and place one hand over your abdomen.
- Feel the abdomen extend out (inhale) and in (exhale).
- Breathe in, make hiss sound using a gentle "SSSS" and sustain for a count of 10. Repeat and relax.
- Breathe in and release "SSSS" for a count of 15. Repeat.
- Gradually build up this controlled release, extending count to 20 and finally 30.
- Keep a steady, consistent outflow of breath.

Periodically Check In

- ✓ Am I breathing rapidly or slowly?
- ✓ Am I taking deep breaths or shallow breaths?
- ✓ Is my breathing pattern uneven or steady?
- ✓ Am I holding my breath?
- ✓ Is my abdomen moving in and out as I breathe?
- ✓ Am I relaxed so I can breathe properly?
- ✓ Are my chest, shoulders, or neck muscles tense?
- ✓ Am I taking deep breaths when I want to reduce anxiety and increase a feeling of calm?
- ✓ Is my posture straight and my breathing relaxed?

Self-Correct

Take control of your breathing and make sure the air you breathe in from the nose goes all the way down to your belly.

Focus for Exercise #4: Speaking Clearly

Form clear and distinct speech sounds. The process of speaking is a complex muscular activity involving the lips, jaw, tongue, soft palate, and facial muscles. It is important to exercise the speech muscles so they can operate efficiently. Clarity in speech is essential because you need listeners to easily hear and understand every word you speak.

Articulators—Lips, Tongue, Jaw, Soft Palate

- Speak slowly enough to accurately form and completely finish each sound.

    Mary made me mash my mushrooms (lips)

    Twenty tentacles tickled Ted (tongue)

    Charlie chews his chocolate (jaw)

    Ricky's sticky yucky duckies (soft palate)

    The lips, the teeth, the tip of the tongue

    You know New York. You need New York. You know you need unique New York.

    All I want is a proper cup of coffee made in a proper coffee pot

    Reading and writing are richly rewarding

    Bill brought a billboard

    Red leather, yellow leather, blue leather

    James just jostled Jean gently

    Please pick up the papers and pile them

    We are all well

Do drop in at the Dewdrop Inn

It's really easy

Keep the closet door closed

A big black bug bit a big black bear

Quickly, quickly, quickly

Literally literary

Cows graze in groves on grass

You asked me to check on this

Thirty thorny thistles thawed throughout

He was gloomy and sluggish

The soup is so delicious

- Enunciate each word of this excerpt from *The Pirates of Penzance* (Gilbert and Sullivan) and breathe at the end of each line:

  I am the very pattern of a modern Major-General;

  I've information vegetable, animal, and mineral;

  I know the Kings of England, and I quote the fights historical,

  From Marathon to Waterloo, in order categorical;

  I'm very well acquainted too with matters mathematical,

  I understand equations, both simple and quadratical,

  About binomial theorem I'm teeming with a lot o' news,

  With many cheerful facts about the square of the hypotenuse.

  I'm very good at integral and differential calculus,

I know the scientific names of beings animalculous,

In short, in matters vegetable, animal, and mineral,

I am the very model of a modern Major-General.

Periodically Check In

✓ Am I articulating my words clearly?

✓ Am I using my lips, tongue, and jaw to create the distinct sounds required for each word?

✓ Am I dropping the ends of words or omitting sounds when I say a word?

✓ Am I speaking too quickly?

✓ Are my words slurred together?

✓ Am I mumbling?

✓ Am I breathing deeply?

✓ Are my shoulders hunched or slouched?

✓ Am I sitting or standing up straight?

Self-Correct

Slow down and open your mouth more to ensure that every word you speak is easily recognized.

Focus for Exercise #5: Varying the Voice

Use changes in the sounds created by the voice to convey meaning. Combining different aspects of sound in speech, such as pitch, volume, pace, and emphasis, affects how messages are heard and understood. Varying your voice keeps listeners interested and engaged.

Pitch

- Speak each sentence all on one pitch—the same high or low sound.

- Say each sentence conversationally and decide which pitch is the highest and lowest.

- Say each sentence with the highest pitch one pitch higher and the low pitch one pitch lower.

- Repeat last step twice more.

> *You said what???*
>
> *It's just not right.*
>
> *I've got a surprise for you.*
>
> *Can I help you?*
>
> *Go to your room.*
>
> *You shouldn't have to do that.*
>
> *That's not very nice.*
>
> *You said you'd help.*
>
> *Can I have some?*

Inflection

- End the question with an upward inflection, and the answer with a downward inflection.

  *One? One. Two? Two. Three? Three. Four? Four.
  Five? Five. Did he like it? Yes. You did? I did. Do it
  now? Do it now. Do you see the point? I see the point.*

Emphasis

- Say the words and phrases in different ways to suggest different meanings.

  Oh—suggest: mild surprise, great surprise,
  indifference, pity, polite interest.

  Why did you do that?—suggest: surprise, accusation,
  anger, despair.

  We are all going—suggest: surprise, defiance,
  disappointment, disgust, sarcasm.

  Why did you do that?—suggest: an inquiry, an
  accusation.

  He was pretty good—suggest: he was really very good,
  he was only fair.

  Okay—suggest: I understand, I'm very disappointed,
  leave me alone, great, enough already.

- Emphasize the italicized words in the sentence

  I didn't say you stole money.

  I ***didn't*** say you stole money.

  I didn't ***say*** you stole money.

  I didn't say ***you*** stole money.

I didn't say you *stole* money.

I didn't say you stole *money*.

Periodically Check In

- ✓ Am I varying the sound of my voice when I speak?
- ✓ Am I using different pitches and tones of voice?
- ✓ Is my speaking pace consistent or varied?
- ✓ Am I using my voice to deliver a clear message?
- ✓ Am I inflecting down at the end of declarative sentences?
- ✓ Is my voice strong, clear, and expressive?
- ✓ Am I overusing force when I convey emphasis?
- ✓ Am I breathing from the diaphragm?
- ✓ Am I maintaining proper posture?

Self-Correct

Increase vocal variety in speech with changes in pitch, tone, and emphasis.

Focus for Exercise #6: Freeing the Voice

Improve voice projection and resonance. Vocal resonators in the body, particularly in the chest, throat, face, nose, and head, give sounds their amplification and distinctive qualities. The more resonators you use, the clearer your voice sounds and the easier your voice projects.

In-Breath, Out-Breath

- Sniff, as though you are picking up a favorite smell in the kitchen, or from a fragrant flower. When sniffing, feel the in-breath through the nose.

- Gasp, with an open mouth, expressing surprise.

- Breathe in, then blow out a candle on the out-breath as actively as possible through the lips. Do this three times, making sure you don't raise your shoulders.

- Sip in air, as though sipping through a straw—5 small sips on 1 inhale, hold, exhale.

- Breathe out fully, then wait. When you can wait no longer, enjoy the in-breath.

Full Value of Vowel Sounds

- Raise and lower the volume as you express different attitudes using one vowel at a time.

- Notice facial expression changes and remember the in-breath.

  Oh?—questioning, commanding, mocking, doubtful, joyful, fearful.

- Focus attention on a spot far away.

- Get your voice to reach the spot as you pull your abdomen in.

- Fully project one word on one breath, lingering on the vowels.

    One! (breathe) *Two!* (breathe) *Three!* (breathe) *Four!* (breathe) *Five!* (breathe).

- Count to 5 on one breath, air flowing smoothly as you pull in abdominal muscles gradually.

Calls and Commands

- Project your voice to make each call.

    Conductor: All aboard.
        A-a-a-all abo-o-o-o-o-a-rd!

    Vendor: Peanuts . . . Popcorn . . . Ice cream . . .
        Beer

    Captain: Ship ahoy!

    Drill Sergeant: Company halt! About face!

    Parent: Stop! Wait for me! Come here!

    Stage Manager: Places everybody . . . Let's go . . .
        Places!

- Project your voice with adequate loudness for each distance.

Next to you:	I can't hear you.
	Ready! Set! Go!
Across the room:	I can't hear you.
	Ready! Set! Go!

Outside the room: I can't hear you.

Ready! Set! Go!

Periodically Check In

- ✓ Am I being heard?
- ✓ Am I using my breath to support my voice?
- ✓ Am I sitting or standing up straight?
- ✓ Am I keeping my body relaxed?
- ✓ Is my voice excessively soft?
- ✓ Am I varying my volume?
- ✓ Am I breathing slowly and deeply?
- ✓ Am I projecting my voice so that my words can be clearly understood?
- ✓ Is my level of vocal energy demonstrating confidence and conviction?

Self-Correct

Stand or sit up straight, breathe deeply, and imagine sending your voice across the room.

Focus for Exercise #7: Speaking with the Body

Use gestures, facial expressions, and purposeful movement to express ideas and feelings. Hand, arm, and face movements add a visual dimension to your communication. They can illustrate or emphasize what you are saying, as well as assist listeners in understanding your intentions, feelings, and messages.

Talking with Your Hands

- Describe two objects—small and big; narrow and wide; up and down—using appropriate gestures. Notice how it feels.

- Describe a vacation, painting a picture of the location with your hands.

- Demonstrate a favorite activity.

- Have a conversation and let your hands gesture naturally.

- Notice how your hands move when you're talking with friends or family, giving directions, making an important point, telling an exciting story, having a heated debate.

Resting Position

- Standing, stretch arms out to the sides.
- Stretch arms straight up, reaching for the sky.
- Close eyes and completely relax your arms, shoulders, hands, head, and neck for 30 seconds.

- Notice when you are completely relaxed, hands rest comfortably at your sides.

Appearing Natural

- Pay attention to particular individuals who appear to communicate naturally, conversationally.
- Notice how they are positioned, either standing or seated.
- Notice how they move their arms and hands for emphasis or to illustrate their points.
- Notice their facial expressions when they speak and when they listen.
- Notice if and when they smile, and how you react to that.
- Notice their eye contact with the people who are listening and people who are speaking.
- Notice the variety in their movements, and how you react to that.
- Identify what makes them engaging and what kind of impact they have on you.

Periodically Check In

- ✓ Am I neglecting to gesture?
- ✓ Are my hands restricted in any way or am I using conversational gestures?
- ✓ Are my gestures reinforcing or illustrating my words?
- ✓ Are my facial expressions conveying my thoughts and feelings?

✓ Are my facial expressions congruent with my words?

✓ Am I smiling all the time or do my facial expressions vary when I speak?

✓ Am I making eye contact when I speak to others?

✓ Am I pacing, moving around too much, or fidgeting out of habit?

✓ Am I sitting or standing up straight rather than slouching or leaning?

Self-Correct

Allow hands to move conversationally, vary facial expressions, and move with purpose.

Focus for Exercise #8: Visualizing

Strategize mentally and imagine yourself engaged in the communication interaction. Engaging in a mental rehearsal is most effective when you create specific images of reality in your mind, including the response you want from others as a result of your interaction. Visualization is a useful technique for improving performance.

Rehearsing by Envisioning

- Sit in a quiet place with eyes closed.

- Picture every detail of the communication interaction, starting from the beginning.

- Imagine the ideal scenario, including how you are confidently and effectively communicating using words, body language, and voice.

- Imagine the others in the interaction responding with interest, nods, or smiles.

- Imagine the overall feeling that you want to have from beginning to end.

- Continue to visualize yourself throughout the interaction and afterward—control the images so that you experience yourself communicating successfully.

Periodically Check In

✓ Am I relaxed and breathing deeply?

✓ Am I mentally placing myself in the interaction?

✓ Am I envisioning myself achieving my desired outcome?

✓ Are all my senses being used to create a mental image of the desired outcome?

✓ Am I envisioning the entire interaction from beginning to end?

✓ Am I imagining how I feel and how others are responding?

✓ Am I visualizing potential challenges and how I overcome those difficulties?

✓ Am I using positive mental imagery to stay focused on success?

✓ Is my mental imagery detailed?

Self-Correct

Create vivid images of the actions you take and the outcomes you achieve.

Focus for Exercise #9: Preparing

Warm up physically and mentally. Before an interaction, take the time to prepare your body and mind so you can start your goal-directed communication from a position of strength. You will experience many benefits: release unnecessary tension, become centered and present, gain control of your breathing, improve focus and concentration.

Do Warm-Up Exercises for Relaxation and Readiness

- Release the shoulders, jaw, lips, and tongue.
- Stretch arms as wide and as tall as you can.
- Center the body.
- Breathe as slowly as you possibly can.
- Do some articulation exercises.

Acquaint Yourself with the Physical Space

- Walk around the space, if possible.
- Sit on the seats where the audience will be sitting.
- Stand or sit in the space where you will be speaking.

Think About the First Moment

- Visualize the first moment in the space.
- Think of the audience as invited guests.

Stay Full of Energy

- Keep breathing, low and slow breaths.

Periodically Check In

- ✓ Am I holding tension in any part of my body?
- ✓ Is my weight evenly distributed throughout my body?
- ✓ Am I breathing slowly and deeply?
- ✓ Am I prepared to clearly articulate every word I speak?
- ✓ Am I ready to use vocal variety to express myself and my ideas?
- ✓ Am I creating vivid, detailed mental images of achieving my desired outcome?
- ✓ Am I envisioning my actions and a positive response from others?
- ✓ Am I aware of my physical surroundings and where I'm positioned in that space?
- ✓ Are my body and mind relaxed?

Self-Correct

Reflect for a few brief moments on your mental and physical state of readiness, and adjust as needed.

Focus for Exercise #10: Observing

Maintain an external focus and pay attention to others. The ability to observe people is critical for effective communicators. Observing the people with whom you are speaking establishes the kind of reciprocal relationship needed for your messages to be received and intended outcomes to be achieved.

Focusing Out

- Choose a situation that allows you to observe a group of people interacting with one another.

- Pay attention to the verbal behavior and interactions—who speaks to whom and for how long, tone of voice, and dialects or language spoken.

- Pay attention to physical behavior and gestures—who interacts with whom and what each person does, who is not interacting, and who gets the most attention from others.

- Maintain your focus on what is actually happening in the group—how people are behaving and reacting, what is being said, and where people are positioned in relation to one another.

Observable Behaviors

- Choose an interview to watch—on television, on video, or in-person.

- Pay attention to the vocal behavior of the interviewer and the interviewee—enunciation, emphasis, tone, speaking rate, and word choice.

- Pay attention to the physical behavior of the interviewer and the interviewee—posture, facial expressions, gestures, eye contact, and body movement.

- Maintain your focus on what is actually happening in the interview—identify any patterns of behavior that you observe in the interviewer or the interviewee.

Periodically Check In

✓ Am I alert?

✓ Is my full attention on observing others?

✓ Are there any distractions that can be eliminated?

✓ Is my attention wandering?

✓ Am I looking but not really seeing because I'm thinking about other things?

✓ Am I concentrating on what I see and what I hear?

✓ Am I noticing micro expressions—brief, involuntary facial expressions that show emotion?

✓ Am I paying attention to visual, vocal, and verbal behavior?

✓ Is there congruence or incongruence in the communication behavior that I'm observing?

Self-Correct

Return to an external focus on others when your focus has gone inward.

Focus for Exercise #11: Describing Details

Choose words that capture interest and convey meaning. Use precise words and provide concrete, specific details to create vivid images in the minds of listeners. Carefully chosen words that appeal to the senses create compelling and memorable messages.

Specific Details, Sensory Language

- Observe the room you're in.

- Describe each item in the room—color, size, shape, markings, location, and any other relevant observable details.

- Observe the clothing that you or others in the room are wearing.

- Describe each item of clothing—color, design, and any other relevant observable details.

- Observe the scene outside the window.

- Describe what you see in as much detail as possible—stick to observable facts, avoid interpreting what you see.

- Observe the details of an item in your possession and describe it in great detail.

- Observe the details of a photo, painting, or picture and describe it in great detail.

- See in your mind's eye a favorite place. Describe it using sensory language, details from the five senses.

- See in your mind's eye a memorable event. Describe it using sensory details.

Periodically Check In

- ✓ Am I choosing my words carefully?
- ✓ Am I speaking in specifics or vague generalities?
- ✓ Are there action words in my sentences?
- ✓ Am I using sensory language in my descriptions?
- ✓ Are my words painting a picture for the listener?
- ✓ Am I speaking slowly enough that the listener can understand every word?
- ✓ Is my meaning clear to the listener?
- ✓ Am I watching how my words are being received by the listener?
- ✓ Am I providing precise and detailed descriptions?

Self-Correct

Select specific, vibrant words to create a picture in the listener's mind.

Focus for Exercise #12: Listening

Concentrate and understand the messaging of others. Developing the ability to listen actively is critical for all effective communicators. It involves focusing attention on the other person, eliminating distractions, restating ideas to confirm understanding, and listening to learn. In conversation, active listeners make the other person feel understood and supported.

Full Awareness

- Choose a situation that requires an extended conversation to better understand an issue.

- Concentrate on what the other person is saying, and refrain from thinking about other things, such as your reply.

- Monitor what you think about while you are listening.

- Make sure you don't respond to distractions, such as your cell phone or computer.

Paraphrase

- Choose a situation that involves a person telling you about a difficult issue.

- Eliminate distractions so you can focus on the speaker.

- Face the other person directly and make eye contact to show interest.

- Listen to learn, observe non-verbal messaging, and occasionally ask clarifying questions.

- Keep an open mind, suspending judgment and not jumping to conclusions.

- Paraphrase, reflect back in your own words the content of one of the speaker's comments to clarify that you have understood them correctly.

- Paraphrase, reflect back the feelings expressed in one of the speaker's comments to signal your full attention and show understanding.

- Paraphrase occasionally, using just a few words to capture the essence of what the speaker said.

Periodically Check In

✓ Are distractions cleared away?

✓ Am I listening to understand the total meaning of the speaker's communication?

✓ Am I paying attention to the speaker's content and feelings?

✓ Am I observing the speaker's non-verbal behavior?

✓ Am I focused on what I want to say instead of actively listening to the whole message?

✓ Am I asking clarifying questions when needed?

✓ Am I paraphrasing what I hear to ensure shared understanding?

✓ Are my paraphrases acknowledged by the listener?

✓ Am I giving the speaker my full attention?

Self-Correct

Listen to understand, observe non-verbal cues, and periodically paraphrase and ask questions.

Focus for Exercise #13: Calming the Mind

Bring awareness to the present moment and acknowledge thoughts and feelings without judgment. Being in the present moment increases self-awareness and awareness of your surroundings. Calming the mind helps put you in a state where you can fully connect and engage with those around you.

Sensory Awareness

- Identify 5 things you hear right now (e.g. cars).
- Identify 5 things you see right now (e.g. clock).
- Identify 5 things you feel right now (e.g. floor).

Breath Count

- Inhale slowly, then exhale slowly. This is one complete breath.
- Continue taking slow, deep breaths. Count each complete breath. Do this for as long as you want.

Body Scan

- Seated, eyes closed, notice the sensation of your feet on floor, legs and back against chair.
- Bring attention to your stomach, letting it soften. Take a breath.
- Notice your hands, arms, neck, throat, jaw, face. Allow them to soften.

- Be aware of your whole body. Keep breathing and relaxing. When ready, open your eyes.

Periodically Check In

- ✓ Am I aware of my breathing?
- ✓ Am I aware of bodily sensations?
- ✓ Am I aware of areas of tension in my body?
- ✓ Am I observing what's around me?
- ✓ Am I listening to the sounds that are present?
- ✓ Am I acknowledging my thoughts right now?
- ✓ Am I acknowledging my feelings right now?
- ✓ Am I experiencing a sense of calm?
- ✓ Am I attentive to the things I'm doing?

Self-Correct

Pay attention to the moment and notice new things.

Focus for Exercise #14: Planning First Words

Carefully craft openings, gain confidence by starting strong, and set the tone with first words. Get the attention of your listeners right away and then make your main point. By planning your first words, you ensure a strong beginning that aligns with your intention.

Attention Grabbers

- Think of a conversational interaction you want to have at work.

- Identify the purpose or objective, relevant issues, and possible action plan.

- Get attention with the unexpected. Consider various attention-grabbing openings, e.g. a question, a surprising statistic, a quote.

- Plan the exact words and then try it out.

- Notice the response to your opening attention-grabber.

Big Ideas

- Think of a conversational interaction you want to have at work.

- Clearly define your big idea—one main message that expresses your unique point of view and what's at stake for the listeners (i.e. why it matters).

- Plan the exact words, one sentence only, and then try it out.

- State your big idea in the beginning and reiterate it in the closing.
- Notice the response of the listeners to your big idea.

Periodically Check In

- ✓ Is my big idea identified?
- ✓ Is my purpose or objective identified?
- ✓ Are the exact words of my opening planned and memorized?
- ✓ Am I grabbing the attention of my listener?
- ✓ Is my opening related to my big idea and purpose?
- ✓ Am I noticing the listener's response to my opening?
- ✓ Am I noticing the listener's response to my big idea?
- ✓ Am I setting the tone with my first words?
- ✓ Is my word choice capturing the listener's interest?

Self-Correct

Select first words to grab attention, set the tone, and capture the listener's interest.

Focus for Exercise #15: Moving from Scripted to Unscripted

Rehearse a presentation without memorizing it word for word. It's more effective to study key concepts than memorize a script. Practice with an outline to help stay on track. Not only will this alleviate the worry of forgetting specific words, it will allow you to deliver your intended message in a conversational style.

Plan-Prepare-Practice

- Plan the opening, body, and ending of your talk (e.g. a toast, a speech, a pitch).
- Write out your script in full sentences.
- Read it aloud several times, word for word.
- Write an outline with the topic sentence and supporting points for each section.
- Practice delivering the talk, glancing at the outline only as needed.
- Repeat this until you know the order of the sections without looking at your notes.
- Write a few bullet points to help you remember the flow of the main points.
- Practice delivering the talk, glancing at the bullet points only as needed.
- Write a few key words to remind you what to cover.
- Practice delivering the talk, glancing at the key words only as needed.
- Repeat this until you can go through the talk without looking at any notes.

Periodically Check In

✓ Am I planning three sections—the beginning, middle, and ending?

✓ Am I preparing to rehearse by writing it out word for word?

✓ Am I starting to practice by reading it aloud?

✓ Am I continuing to prepare and practice using bullet points only?

✓ Am I practicing over and over so that I only need key words as reminders?

✓ Am I ready to practice without any notes?

✓ Am I practicing without notes as many times as possible?

✓ Are my first words planned and memorized?

✓ Am I comfortable with the content so I can talk conversationally and focus on the listeners?

Self-Correct

Focus your attention on talking conversationally to listeners and watching them receive your message.

Focus for Exercise #16: Shortening Sentences

Be concise. Express your desired message in as few words as possible. Improve your communication effectiveness by using shorter, simpler sentences.

Features and Benefits

- Select a product or a service to describe.
- Identify specific features of the product or service.
- State each feature in one short sentence.
- Identify the benefits of the product or service—the value they give to you or others.
- State each benefit in one short sentence.

Sentence Examples

- Use the word "speak" or "spoke" in as many 2-word sentences as you can think of in a minute. Notice how much meaning you can convey using short sentences.
- Use the word "speak" or "spoke" in as many 3-word sentences as you can think of in a minute. Notice how much meaning you can convey using short sentences.
- Continue the process, using either "speak" or "spoke" in 4-word sentences, 5-word sentences, 6-word sentences, and on up to 10-word sentences.

- Practice speaking to someone using short sentences. Notice how much meaning you can convey using only the essential words.

Periodically Check In

- ✓ Am I grabbing the attention of listeners with a concise opening sentence?
- ✓ Am I focusing on what matters to the listeners?
- ✓ Am I limiting each sentence to one main idea?
- ✓ Am I expressing myself, my intent, and my thoughts with as few words as possible?
- ✓ Am I choosing my words carefully and watching how they're received by the listeners?
- ✓ Am I eliminating run-on sentences?
- ✓ Are my sentences short and easy for listeners to follow?
- ✓ Are my short sentences powerful?
- ✓ Are my short sentences repeatable?

Self-Correct

Eliminate every non-essential word.

Focus for Exercise #17: Establishing Connection

Practice talking to a group, establishing and sustaining connection with one person at a time. Talking to one person at a time makes each person feel connected. This is a highly effective way to engage your audience, and make your delivery more personal and conversational.

Complete Thoughts and Pauses

- Gather three or more friends or colleagues to assist you and make sure they understand the purpose of the exercise.

- Pick a topic that you can comfortably talk about for two minutes.

- Establish a connection with one audience member before you begin to speak.

- Keep paying full attention to that audience member while you complete one thought. Pause and watch the message land on that person.

- Find another pair of eyes, and establish a connection with another audience member before beginning a new thought.

- Pay full attention to that second audience member while you complete a thought. Pause and watch the message land on that person.

- Repeat this pattern throughout the two-minute presentation.

- Elicit feedback from the audience members.

- Use the same two-minute presentation and repeat the process of establishing and sustaining connection with one person at a time for a complete thought.

- Repeat the feedback process. Elicit feedback from the audience members and then offer your own observations.

Periodically Check In

✓ Am I relaxed, aligned, and breathing properly?

✓ Am I attending to one person at a time?

✓ Am I saying one complete, short sentence to one person?

✓ Am I watching my message land on that person?

✓ Am I allowing silence, pausing after each sentence and before starting the next one?

✓ Am I repeating the process of speaking one complete thought to one person at a time?

✓ Am I establishing a connection with a person before speaking?

✓ Am I maintaining the connection and staying focused on that person until the sentence ends?

✓ Am I incorporating the feedback?

Self-Correct

In a state of relaxed awareness, connect with one listener at a time and make sure you clearly convey your message to the individuals in the group.

Focus for Exercise #18: Speaking with Purpose

Practice identifying clear intentions and explore how different intentions impact others. First, identify what you want as a result of the interaction; then, keep that intention in mind throughout the interaction. You increase the effectiveness of your communication with a clearly defined intention.

Action Verbs

- Gather three or more friends or colleagues to assist you and make sure they understand the objective of the exercise.

- Think about a topic and your focus. Then select three action verbs that describe your purpose. Be specific about your intended outcome. (For example, you may want to *persuade*—get them to do something specific as a result of your talk; *inform*—get them to know specific things as a result of your talk; *teach*—enable them to do something specific as a result of your talk; or you may want to *entertain* or *inspire* the listeners.)

- Speak for two minutes, focusing on one of your intentions.

- Elicit feedback. Ask the audience members what response they had after having listened to your talk. If they received what you intended, let them know that this was your intention. If they did not, do it again, seeking to convey the same intention more strongly.

- Deliver approximately the same talk two more times. Focus on a different intention each time.

- Repeat the feedback process, eliciting feedback from the audience members and let them know what you intended.

- End the practice with an assessment of your strengths in communicating a clear intention and how you want to continue developing this skill.

Periodically Check In

✓ Am I identifying a clear intention?

✓ Am I conveying my intention clearly?

✓ Am I incorporating the feedback?

✓ Am I using concise, precise verbal messaging?

✓ Is my visual, vocal, and verbal communication congruent?

✓ Is my vocal and physical presence strong?

✓ Am I attending to individuals when I speak?

✓ Am I connecting with individuals when I speak?

✓ Is my delivery conversational?

Self-Correct

Identify and keep in mind what you want the listeners to know, feel, or do as a result of your communication.

Focus for Exercise #19: Structuring Effectively

Practice crafting a story using a simple three-part structure. Stories are compelling platforms for conveying ideas because they can engage the imagination, elicit emotional responses, and move people into action. By adhering to the basic three-part structure of beginning-middle-end, you make your story memorable and easy for listeners to follow.

Narrative Accounts of Events

- First, set the scene in the beginning. Include details that help listeners imagine the situation—when, who, where.

- Second, set up the tension in the middle. Include the context, conflict or challenge, contrast between what is and what could be, what the emotions are, what is at stake.

- Third, resolve the tension in the ending. Include actions taken to bridge the gap between what is and what could be, and what the results and benefits are.

- Highlight the key takeaway in the close.

- Consider other stories you can use to illustrate a concept or idea or move others to action.

- Tell stories. Notice the emotional responses you get. Ask listeners if the stories engaged their imagination.

Periodically Check In

✓ Is there a beginning, middle, and ending to my story?

✓ Am I grabbing the listener's attention in the beginning?

✓ Am I providing supporting details in the middle?

✓ Am I using sensory language to create a vivid description?

✓ Is my closing message clear and memorable?

✓ Am I eliciting the intended response?

✓ Am I attending to listeners when I tell the story?

✓ Is my connection with listeners maintained throughout the story?

✓ Am I incorporating feedback from listeners?

Self-Correct

Structure your story so that you can move the listeners from where they are at the beginning to where you want them to be at the ending.

Focus for Exercise #20: Speaking Conversationally

Practice delivering ideas in a conversational way. Speaking in a conversational style puts you and your listeners at ease. It's easier for people to listen to you when your delivery sounds natural. Create conversational interactions to reach a mutual understanding and to achieve desired outcomes within a reciprocal relationship.

Make It a Conversation

Version 1

- Ask a friend, family member, or colleague to assist you and make sure they understand the objective of the exercise.

- Find a magazine or newspaper article that interests you.

- Read a paragraph out loud.

- Read each sentence of that paragraph to yourself, and then say that sentence in a conversational way to the other person. Paraphrase, if necessary, to get the point across conversationally.

- Notice the difference between reciting and speaking conversationally.

Version 2

- Find a written speech and read a paragraph out loud.

- Read each sentence to yourself, and then say that sentence to the other person as if you were having a conversation. Make sure to keep your tone conversational throughout.

- Notice the difference between reciting and speaking conversationally.

Version 3

- Identify a talk that you have to give—opening remarks at a meeting, event, product introduction, training session, social function, interview, or other work contexts.

- Practice delivering those remarks, keeping your tone conversational throughout.

- Elicit feedback. Ask the participants what response they had to your conversational style of delivery.

Periodically Check In

✓ Am I speaking the same as I do when I have conversations with friends?

✓ Is there vocal variety when I speak?

✓ Is my voice projecting and my pace moderate?

✓ Am I clearly enunciating every word and pausing at the ends of sentences?

✓ Am I maintaining good posture when I speak?

✓ Am I using natural, conversational gestures when I speak?

✓ Am I identifying and conveying my intention?

✓ Am I establishing and maintaining a connection with one listener at a time?

✓ Am I incorporating the feedback from listeners about my IMPACT?

Self-Correct

Maintain a conversational style throughout your communication interactions with individuals and groups.

Conclusion

Focused practice yields results.

This chapter details discrete skills to practice. It first isolates the skill so it can be mastered, and then sets us up to apply these skills throughout the day in situations at work.

It is worth noting that some of these practice activities, such as speaking in short sentences or maintaining eye contact with one person for one complete thought, may seem "hard" or "unnatural" at first. I can say from years of experience that with continual practice, these exercises become easier and easier to do. Eventually, they feel completely natural.

Keep in mind that each curated exercise has a definite purpose. Some require practicing alone, some require practicing with other people. All the skills that we practice in these exercises strengthen our ability to be effective communicators who can achieve desired outcomes and maximize impact during communication interactions.

Read on for ways to keep your focused communication practice alive, effective, and ongoing.

6

COMMUNICATE WITH IMPACT

Having become familiar with the paradigm principles and having done some of the 20 IMPACT Exercises, we now consider different ways to put them into action. Getting better at communicating with impact is within our reach. It takes practice.

"How should I practice?" This is a question I'm often asked by professionals who want to improve their communication effectiveness: knowing how to practice is critically important for achieving results.

In this chapter, we will focus on six ways to design and execute effective IMPACT practice. These practice approaches are: 1—Isolate a Skill; 2—Combine Skills; 3—Self-Assess; 4—Self-Correct; 5—Integrate Feedback; 6—Persist and Progress. Then we will recap the benefits of engaging in IMPACT practice to improve our communication effectiveness.

Practice Approach 1: Isolate a Skill

Working on a skill in isolation is a type of practice activity specifically designed to improve performance. After deciding which skill to work on, there must be a lot of repeated practice of that particular skill.

- Step one: identify an aspect of IMPACT that you want to improve.
- Step two: isolate one particular skill to work on mastering.
- Step three: practice it over and over.

Consider, for example, vocal presence. There are many aspects of vocal presence that can be enhanced, including breath control, diction, and vocal variety. Let's select one of the basic vocal skills to improve—vocal projection. We can break this down into smaller chunks. Vocal projection requires releasing tension, breathing deeply, and freeing the voice. To practice this discrete skill in isolation, see IMPACT Exercises 2, 3, and 6 in Chapter 5. Repeat exercises often.

Another example of an individual skill to practice might be posture if we want to enhance our physical presence. Proper alignment is an extremely important aspect of physical presence. It not only affects how we come across, it also significantly influences how we use our bodies when we express our thoughts and feelings. Practicing this discrete skill involves finding center and releasing tension. Refer to IMPACT Exercises 1 and 2 in Chapter 5 for specific instructions. Focused practice to develop a particular skill requires effort and concentration.

Isolating specific aspects of what we do and focusing on getting better at just those things is highly effective for skill development. It allows us to build muscle memory and strengthens our ability to achieve maximum impact when we communicate at work.

Practice Approach 2: Combine Skills

Combining skills is a type of practice activity that takes place in conversation. After practicing isolated skills, we use them with other skills in real situations.

- Step one: before, choose the situation in which you will apply the skills.
- Step two: during, pay attention to how you apply the skills.
- Step three: after, reflect on what worked well and what could be improved.

There are opportunities to integrate communication skills in everyday situations. Take, for example, the basic skill of making eye contact, along with the skills of observing and listening to others during our communication interactions. Noticing what we're doing, when we're doing it, and what we're paying attention to during a conversation is extremely informative. Refer to IMPACT Exercises 10, 12, and 17 in Chapter 5.

This type of practice requires both planning and a high degree of specificity. To design a successful practice plan for combining skills requires careful selection of the situation and the skills to be used during the conversation.

Designing practice that takes place in conversation enables us to learn what yields results in actual interactions so we can then apply these skills when we communicate at work to achieve intended outcomes.

Practice Approach 3: Self-Correct

An excellent way to get better at communicating effectively with maximum impact is to self-correct in real time. This involves awareness and action. Initially, we become aware of our own communication behavior by reflecting *in* action, critically assessing actions as they are taken. Following this, we make whatever minor adjustment in our communication behavior is needed to increase our effectiveness. (This is not the same as reflecting *on* action, thinking back on an action that was taken.)

- Step one: attend to how you show up, what cues you send, and how you hold your intention.

- Step two: adjust a specific aspect of your verbal, vocal, or visual communication, as needed.

- Step three: stay focused on intent as you make the minor behavioral adjustment in real time.

Strategic communicators not only notice the responses they are getting, but what they are doing to get those responses. They adjust their behavior on the spot, as needed, to achieve desired results during their communication interactions.

For example, consider the common challenge of speaking more slowly. Changing from a fast speaking pace to a more moderate one takes continual practice. It is not easy to change this long-standing habit but we can do it with focused attention, repeated practice, and a strong commitment to speaking more clearly. Refer to IMPACT Exercise 4 in Chapter 5. Recall the competence model of moving from unconscious incompetence to unconscious competence.

At the conscious competence stage, when we are able to use the skill but only with effort, we may catch ourselves speeding up, perhaps from excitement or reverting back to a pace that's been used for years. Notice this and then self-correct.

We can engage in real-time reflection during any communication interaction and we can self-correct whatever aspect of IMPACT we want to improve. For each of the 20 IMPACT Exercises in Chapter 5, there is a suggestion for how to self-correct.

Practice Approach 4: Self-Assess

Whether practicing a skill in isolation or practicing combining skills in daily interactions, we benefit from self-assessment. This, in essence, is an after action review of our practice activity.

- Step one: consider your planned practice activity.
- Step two: assess what worked.
- Step three: identify what could work better next time.

Video and audio technology can also be used to self-assess a practice activity. After doing a practice activity and recording it, watch the video or listen to the audio:

- Step one: identify all the things that you liked about how you did the practice activity.
- Step two: describe the elements you didn't like using objective, non-judgmental language.
- Step three: select one or two things you want to work on improving and identify an improvement strategy for each.

Continual assessment supports continual improvement. Ask yourself a series of questions: What did I set out to improve?

What was my plan to achieve this? What did I learn? What, specifically, went well and why? What could have gone better? What's next for my practice?

Action and reflection on our action is a powerful way to learn. After practicing any of the IMPACT Exercises described in Chapter 5, self-assess. After engaging in any communication, whether it's a one-to-one, small group or large group interaction, self-assess. Invest time in self-assessing what went well and where there is room for improvement to ensure that the practice is efficient and transferable to situations at work.

We may choose to implement and assess practice that focuses on how we use our body to communicate, which in turn affects our state of mind when we communicate. Similarly, we may choose to implement and assess practice that focuses on mindset, which influences how we use our body to communicate. The reality is that we are an integrated system and can make significant improvements by making small adjustments.

Practice Approach 5: Integrate Feedback

Receiving feedback and incorporating it into our practice activity is crucial for getting better at communicating with impact. When people ask me how they can get feedback, my response is always the same: "Ask for it." After we receive feedback, repeat the practice, integrating the feedback.

- Step one: identify a feedback provider, and tell that person exactly what you want feedback on.
- Step two: do the practice activity and receive feedback.
- Step three: repeat the practice using the feedback and notice its effect.

Getting feedback on our communication is helpful because it lets us know the impact of our behavior on another person. Eliciting feedback is an essential component of IMPACT Exercises 17, 18, 19, and 20 in Chapter 5. It can be applied to all the IMPACT Exercises. Just ask someone to be a feedback provider. The feedback content should focus on what has been seen, not on personal characteristics. After receiving feedback, put it to use. Redo the practice integrating the feedback and notice whether it improves the practice.

It is best to let the feedback provider know what we are working on so the feedback is specific to what we are trying to learn or accomplish. Ask for behavioral feedback (a description of observable behavior), specific feedback (a description of one specific instance of observable behavior and its impact on the feedback provider), and balanced feedback (what the feedback provider thinks worked well and what could be improved).

When receiving feedback, listen carefully, stay open, and restate the feedback to confirm understanding. Effective feedback allows us to see the results of our practice through another person's eyes. We also gain insights into our practice activity that can inform what we work on moving forward.

Practice Approach 6: Persist and Progress

Staying motivated is a critical part of practice. We are all capable of designing and executing a practice activity to achieve our desired goals. Acknowledging each small win—even simply making the effort to engage in practice—motivates us to continue.

- Step one: decide what to practice, how to practice, and when to practice.
- Step two: practice and practice some more.
- Step three: acknowledge incremental progress.

Practice takes effort. Our choice to expend effort on practice activity and persist with that effort is strengthened by acknowledging incremental progress. We can design and execute effective IMPACT practice to get better at things we want to improve, and to reinforce things we already do well. The more we experience a sense of progress, the more likely we are to continue our practice to improve communication effectiveness.

We have countless opportunities to engage in IMPACT practice. Most of us have probably practiced using parts of the paradigm in communication interactions at work, perhaps in a meeting, a workplace conversation, a presentation, or a speech. Now we have one cohesive system to assist us in using all parts of the paradigm in all our one-on-one, small group and large group strategic communication interactions.

Here is a recap of the basic parts of the IMPACT Paradigm:

 ## Intending:

Focus on Intending to Achieve Desired Outcomes

Every time we communicate, we affect the people with whom we are communicating. Therefore, it is critically important to determine the specific response we want. It could relate to what they know, how they feel, or ways they act.

We begin the process of communication with intending—knowing the effect we want to cause in others and setting that as a goal for each interaction. By beginning with the end in mind and remaining focused on our intent throughout the communication, we significantly increase the likelihood of achieving our desired outcomes.

 **Messaging:**

Make Messaging Memorable with Congruent Visual, Vocal, and Verbal Communication

We convey our thoughts and feelings using three modes of expression—body, voice, and words. To make an impact, we need to make sure that our visual, vocal, and verbal communication all support each other.

Our visual communication is what others see. We convey our messages through body language, including head movements, facial expressions, hand gestures, physical posture, muscle tensions, and breathing patterns. Our vocal communication is how we sound to others. Paralanguage, the non-verbal elements of speech that convey shades of meaning, include pace, pitch, volume, intonation, emphasis, pauses, and articulation. Our verbal communication is the words we choose to say. When we create and send congruent verbal and non-verbal messages, we can effectively share memorable content with others.

 Presence:

Be Present to Enable Full Expression

We can think of presence as how we show up, including how we hold physical space and how we hold attention with our voice. In the IMPACT Paradigm, presence involves using our body, voice, and words to fully express ourselves. A core assumption is that we are capable of taking actions that move us toward the goal of developing to our fullest expression of self.

All parts of the IMPACT Paradigm contribute to our ability to harness the power of our presence. We can enhance our presence with awareness, physical stamina, and engagement in the core communication practices.

 ## Attending:

Attend to Others to Create Connection

When we give all of our physical and cognitive attention to other people, they respond in kind. Our focus of attention—one person at a time—signals we are invested in having that person get our message and engage with us in a meaningful interaction.

Attending establishes the communication as an interactive process. It is our external focus on others that enables us to establish the relational aspect that is needed for purposeful communication.

 ## Connecting:

Connect Throughout the Communication to Maximize Impact

For strategic communication to be effective, it is vitally important to get others to pay attention, to continue to pay attention, and fully engage with us and our message. We can create a firm connection, what I refer to as a non-negotiable connection with others, by using the attending and connecting parts of the paradigm. It is crucial to both establish and maintain this kind of non-negotiable connection because it secures involvement in the communication interaction.

Attending and connecting are two essential parts of the IMPACT Paradigm because they ensure mutual engagement, a necessary aspect of communicating with impact to achieve desired outcomes.

 **Together:**

Create a Conversational Interaction, Together

Conversation is derived from Latin words that mean "to move together." By moving together, we build relationships, share information, exchange ideas, and make decisions with others. It is through conversation that we create shared meaning, reach outcomes, and take informed action, together.

In the IMPACT Paradigm, we approach strategic communication as a conversational interaction that is engaging, dynamic, and collaborative.

A Final Word

All of us can communicate with IMPACT. We now understand each part of the IMPACT Paradigm. We can practice using the approaches outlined in this chapter. We can apply the paradigm on a daily basis.

Congratulations to all who want to improve communication effectiveness and already took action by reading this book. The key to continually improving communication effectiveness is to use all parts of the IMPACT Paradigm when we engage in conversational interactions at work. Spend some time reflecting on what's working well and what can be improved moving forward. Keep practicing, keep engaging, and enjoy the process of communicating purposefully with impact and achieving desired outcomes.

REFERENCES

Abercrombie, David. 1968. Paralanguage. *International Journal of Language and Communication Disorders*, *3*(1): 55–59.

von Bertalanffy, Ludwig. 1950. An Outline of General System Theory. *The British Journal for the Philosophy of Science*, *1*(2): 134–165.

Birdwhistell, Ray L. 1970. *Kinesics and Context: Essays on Body Motion Communication*. Philadelphia, PA: University of Pennsylvania Press.

Bolton, Robert. 1979. *People Skills: How to Assert Yourself, Listen to Others, and Resolve Conflicts*. Englewood Cliffs, NJ: Prentice-Hall.

Cuddy, Amy. 2012. Your Body Language May Shape Who You Are. Retrieved from www.ted.com/talks/amy_cuddy_your_body_language_shapes_who_you_are

——. 2015. *Presence: Bringing Your Boldest Self to Your Biggest Challenges*. New York: Little Brown and Company.

Dweck, Carol S. 2006. *Mindset: The New Psychology of Success*. New York: Ballantine Books.

Einstein, Albert. 1934. On the Method of Theoretical Physics, a Herbert Spence Lecture, Oxford. *Philosophy of Science*, *1*(2): 163–169.

Ekman, Paul. 2009. Become Versed in Reading Faces. Entrepreneur. doi: 200934. Retrieved from www.entrepreneur.com/article/200934#

Ericsson, K. Anders, Ralf Th. Krampe, and Clemens Tesch-Romer. 1993. The Role of Deliberate Practice in the Acquisition of Expert Performance. *Psychological Review*, *100*(3): 363–406.

Goleman, Daniel. 1997. *Emotional Intelligence: Why It Can Matter More Than IQ*. New York: Bantam.

——. 2006. *Social Intelligence: The Revolutionary New Science of Human Relationships*. New York: Bantam.

Hall, Edward T. 1966. *The Hidden Dimension*. New York: Doubleday.

——. 1973. *The Silent Language*. New York: Anchor Books.

——. 1976. *Beyond Culture*. New York: Anchor Books/Doubleday.

Horton, William S. 2012. Shared Knowledge, Mutual Understanding and Meaning Negotiation. In *Cognitive Pragmatics*, ed. Hans-Jorg Schmid, 375–404. Berlin/Boston: de Gruyter Mouton.

Iacoboni, Marco. 2008. *Mirroring People: The New Science of How We Connect with Others*. New York: Farrar, Straus and Giroux.

Kahn, William. 1992. To Be Fully There: Psychological Presence at Work. *Human Relations*, *45*(4): 321–349.

Kuhn, Thomas S. 1962. The Structure of Scientific Revolutions. Chicago, IL: The University of Chicago Press.

McCaskey, Michael B. 1979. The Hidden Messages Managers Send. *Harvard Business Review*, *57*(6): 135–148.

Mehrabian, Albert. 1971. *Silent Messages*. Belmont, CA: Wadsworth Publishing Company.

Patton, Michael Quinn. 1990. Qualitative Evaluation and Research Methods, 2nd ed. Thousand Oaks, CA: Sage Publications.

Siegel, Daniel J. 2007. *The Mindful Brain: Reflection and Attunement in the Cultivation of Well-Being*. New York: W.W. Norton & Company.

Society for Neuroscience. 2012. Hormones: Communication between the Brain and the Body. Retrieved from www.brainfacts.org/brain-basics/cell-communication/articles/2012/hormones-communication-between-the-brain-and-the-body

Stark, Mallory. 2004. Surfacing Your Underground Organization. Harvard Business School Working Knowledge. doi: 4456. Retrieved from https://hbswk.hbs.edu/archive/surfacing-your-underground-organization

Su, Amy Jen and Muriel Maignan Wilkins. 2013. *Own the Room: Discover Your Signature Voice to Master Your Leadership Presence*. Boston, MA: Harvard Business Review Press.

Turkle, Sherry. 2015. *Reclaiming Conversation: The Power of Talk in a Digital Age*. New York: Penguin Press.

Watzlawick, Paul, Janet Beavin Bavelas and Don D. Jackson. 1967. *Pragmatics of Human Communication: A Study of Interactional Patterns, Pathologies, and Paradoxes*. New York: W.W. Norton & Company.

INDEX

CPSIA information can be obtained
at www.ICGtesting.com
Printed in the USA
FFHW012110051218
49756654-54225FF